THE POCKET IDIOT'S GUIDE TO

Poker Bets and Bluffs

by David Apostolico

ALPHA

A member of Penguin Group (USA) Inc.

ALPHA BOOKS

Published by the Penguin Group

Penguin Group (USA) Inc., 375 Hudson Street, New York, New York 10014, U.S.A.

Penguin Group (Canada), 10 Alcorn Avenue, Toronto, Ontario, Canada M4V 3B2 (a division of Pearson Penguin Canada Inc.)

Penguin Books Ltd, 80 Strand, London WC2R 0RL, England

Penguin Ireland, 25 St Stephen's Green, Dublin 2, Ireland (a division of Penguin Books Ltd)

Penguin Group (Australia), 250 Camberwell Road, Camberwell, Victoria 3124, Australia (a division of Pearson Australia Group Pty Ltd)

Penguin Books India Pvt Ltd, 11 Community Centre, Panchsheel Park, New Delhi—110 017, India

Penguin Group (NZ), cnr Airborne and Rosedale Roads, Albany, Auckland 1310, New Zealand (a division of Pearson New Zealand Ltd)

Penguin Books (South Africa) (Pty) Ltd, 24 Sturdee Avenue, Rosebank, Johannesburg 2196, South Africa

Penguin Books Ltd, Registered Offices: 80 Strand, London WC2R 0RL, England

International Standard Book Number: 978-1-59257-647-0
Library of Congress Catalog Card Number: 2007922825

09   08   07   8   7   6   5   4   3   2   1

Interpretation of the printing code: The rightmost number of the first series of numbers is the year of the book's printing; the rightmost number of the second series of numbers is the number of the book's printing. For example, a printing code of 07-1 shows that the first printing occurred in 2007.

Note: This publication contains the opinions and ideas of its author. It is intended to provide helpful and informative material on the subject matter covered. It is sold with the understanding that the author and publisher are not engaged in rendering professional services in the book. If the reader requires personal assistance or advice, a competent professional should be consulted.

The author and publisher specifically disclaim any responsibility for any liability, loss, or risk, personal or otherwise, which is incurred as a consequence, directly or indirectly, of the use and application of any of the contents of this book.

Most Alpha books are available at special quantity discounts for bulk purchases for sales promotions, premiums, fund-raising, or educational use. Special books, or book excerpts, can also be created to fit specific needs.

For details, write: Special Markets, Alpha Books, 375 Hudson Street, New York, NY 10014.

Contents

Introduction

Poker has long been an American institution. From Friday night home games to big televised championship events, players of all stripes try their hands at this time-honored game. No matter what your level of experience, there is a game waiting for you.

Poker is a game of skill but it is a complex one. On its surface, the basic rules of play are rather simple and easy to grasp. What separates the winners from the losers, however, is the winner's ability to master all of the subtle nuances of the game. Knowing when to bet and how much to bet are keys to maximizing profit. It's not enough to win a hand if you didn't extract as much money as you should have.

Of course, bluffing and other forms of deception are an integral part of the game as well. Bluffing is an art form that must be used sparingly and under the right conditions. Poker is a game of finding small edges and exploiting those edges. In this book, we'll provide you with all of the tools necessary to bet your hands for profit, bluff under the most optimal conditions, and turn you into a winning player. Let's get to it so you can start using these skills at the poker table.

Using This Book

In addition to the main text, this book includes
sidebars, each with a distinctive visual cue:

Definition

These sidebars include definitions of
terms you are likely to hear when you
sit down to the poker table.

Hold 'em

These are strategic tips to help you
play your hand for maximum value.

Fold 'em

These warnings point common pitfalls
to avoid so you can hold onto your
chips.

The Gutshot Straight

These sidebars highlight poker lore and
advanced strategy.

Acknowledgments

I would like to thank my agent, Sheree Bykofsky, for dealing me a winning hand and hooking me up with the great people at Alpha Books. I also would like to thank a number of people at Alpha: Marie Butler-Knight, Mike Sanders, Billy Fields, Paul Dinas, Nancy Lewis, Kayla Dugger, and Amy Borrelli.

Finally, my biggest thanks and gratitude goes out to my wife, Cindy, and my boys Evan, Ryan, and Derek, who encourage, support, and provide never-ending inspiration. It's not hard to shrug off a bad beat when I know I get to come home to such a wonderful family.

Trademarks

All terms mentioned in this book that are known to be or are suspected of being trademarks or service marks have been appropriately capitalized. Alpha Books and Penguin Group (USA) Inc. cannot attest to the accuracy of this information. Use of a term in this book should not be regarded as affecting the validity of any trademark or service mark.

Chapter

The Purpose of Poker

In This Chapter

- Make the right choice
- Win money, not pots
- A chip saved is a chip earned
- Using deception
- Getting started

Poker is a game that combines skill and luck. If you play long enough, the luck should even out among the players and the winners will prove to be the most skillful. Presumably, you play poker because you think you're better than your opponents. If you're not, then perhaps you're reading this book to improve your play so you can consistently beat the regulars in your game.

The good news is that you're in the right place. This book is all about improving your win percentage by maximizing the value out of your play. I caution, however, that it won't be simple. Poker is an easy game to learn but a difficult one to master. It is a nuanced game that is very dependent on the situation. If you can develop a solid foundation of proper betting and bluffing habits, you will be well on your way to beating the game.

Hold 'em

Beginning players tend to greatly over-estimate the amount of bluffing being done at the poker table. Bluffing is a critical part of the game but experienced players don't bluff nearly as much as beginning players believe.

Our goal is to teach you when to *bet*, when to *fold*, when to *raise*, and when to *bluff*. To paraphrase Kenny Rogers, you have to know when to hold 'em and when to fold 'em. That's only the beginning of the equation, though. You also have to know when to bet for maximum value and when to put on the brakes. Finally, you need to know how to bluff to win some pots you otherwise would not win.

To put the importance of this in perspective, let's take a hypothetical game of 10 players in a game of no-limit Texas Hold 'em. After 10 hands are dealt, each player has won one pot. Do you think each player will have won the same amount of money?

The answer is no. Now, let's take the hypothetical one step forward. Let's say that every single hand was dealt identically and every player got to play the hand from each position with the cards dealt to that position. Again, do you think each player will have won the same amount at the end of the 10 hands? Again, the answer is no. The answer is no because not everyone plays their hands the same way. Some players will be more adept at extracting extra chips from their hands than others, while some players will be better adept at minimizing their losses. By the end of this book, our goal is to make sure you are the player with the most chips after our 10 hypothetical hands.

Fold 'em

It doesn't pay to be overly cynical in poker. If you assume your opponents are bluffing, it could cost you a lot of chips. Even if you believe an opponent is bluffing, it's dangerous to call if you don't have at least a decent hand.

Since no-limit Texas Hold 'em is the game of choice in most poker circles, we'll be using it as our reference point. The concepts learned will be applicable to any game. If you're new to the game or you need a refresher, there's a Texas Hold 'em Primer at the end of this chapter. When making references to sample hands, suits will be designated as follows: s for spades, c for clubs, d for diamonds, and h for hearts.

Do the Right Thing

Legendary poker player, author, and teacher Mike Caro famously used to begin his lectures with the question "What is the objective of poker?" Routinely, the answers would be some derivation of "to win money." While that answer may be the ultimate goal, Caro felt strongly that it wasn't the objective of poker. To paraphrase, the objective of poker is to make correct decisions.

That's sound advice and a good place for us to start. If you concentrate on the process and not the result, the money will eventually flow your way in the long run. Poker is a fickle game and the luck factor can play a crucial role in the short term. If you concentrate on making correct decisions, then you can divorce yourself from the role of luck.

You Can Do Everything Right but Win

There will be plenty of times when you make the correct decision and you lose the pot. That's the nature of poker. You can play a hand perfectly, betting all the way with the best hand and making it unwise for your opponent to call. Then your opponent happens to *suck out* on you by making his *gutshot* straight on the *river*. *Bad beats* like this are part of the game, so it's better to get used to them than to get upset over them.

Definition

To **suck out** is to hit a card that helps you make the winning hand when you are a big underdog.

A **gutshot** is an inside straight draw. An inside straight draw is when only a card of one rank will make your straight (i.e., you have 4, 5, 6, and 8 and need a 7 to make your straight).

The fifth and final community card in Hold 'em is considered the **river**.

A **bad beat** is when you have a strong hand beaten by an opponent who was a big underdog but makes a lucky draw. This is especially true when your opponent is playing poorly and should not have been in the pot in the first place.

You Can Do Everything Right and Expect to Lose

That's right. Sometimes, you will make a *call* fully expecting to lose and it will be the correct decision. For instance, say you have the *nut flush draw* on the *turn*. You know you are about a 4–1 underdog to win the hand. Yet, there is $70 in the pot and it will cost you $10 to call. You are getting 7–1 odds to call when you are only a 4–1 underdog. The correct decision is to call the bet even though you know you are likely to lose the hand.

If you consistently call bets when you have favorable pot odds, you will make money in the long run. You will make that flush one out of five times, and when you do, the money you will win will more than make up for the times you lost making that same call.

Hopefully, you are starting to see why it's more important to make correct decisions than anything else you do at the table. Correct decisions will lead to long-term profits.

> **Definition**_____
>
> When you **call,** you place in the pot an amount of chips equal to an opponent's bet or raise.
>
> The **nut flush draw** is having a draw to the best possible flush. For example, if you hold KhQh and the board has Ah9h2d, any heart will give you the nut flush.
>
> The **turn** is the fourth card on the board and is dealt after the betting round following the flop concludes.

The Rule of Four

Knowing pot odds and outs is essential if you are going to make correct decisions. We strongly suggest that you study Appendix B, a chart of Texas Hold 'em odds and outs. An *out* is a card that will improve your hand to a winning one. For example, if you have Ah8h and the flop comes 2h4hKd, then any heart will give you the nut flush and, in all probability, the winning hand. Since you have two hearts in your hand and two more are on the *board*, then there are still nine more hearts remaining.

Definition

When a player is behind in a hand but can make a winning hand if the right cards come, those right cards that make his winning hand are called **outs**. A hand of 9s10s with a flop of As7d4s has nine outs (the nine remaining spades) that can make a flush.

The five community cards placed in the center of the table are known as the **board**.

An easy way to calculate odds on the flop is by the rule of four. With the rule of four, you multiply the number of your outs by four to arrive at the percentage chance you will see one of your outs. In this case, $9 \times 4 = 36$. So you have approximately a 36 percent chance of making your flush by the river. The actual odds are closer to 35 percent, but the rule of four is a quick way to get a real close approximation.

A corollary of the rule of four is the rule of two. After the turn, you can calculate your odds using a multiplier of two instead of four. In our example, if the turn does not bring a heart, then the odds of making the flush on the river are now calculated as nine (your number of outs) multiplied by two. So you have approximately an 18 percent chance of making the flush (the real odds are just slightly higher but this is close enough).

Know the Math, Use Psychology

Poker is both an art and a science. If you are going to consistently make correct decisions, you need to know the math cold. When the math becomes second nature, you will be well positioned to win the psychological battles at the poker table. In later chapters, we'll look in depth at bluffing and other forms of deception. In order to properly implement those strategies, you will need a strong grasp of the underlying math.

Ignore Short-Term Results

A common mistake of both beginning and experienced players is to put too much emphasis on the most recent results. They overadjust based on a few hands. Win a few hands and all of a sudden, a player thinks he's invincible. He's playing every hand believing he can't lose.

Lose a few tough hands and a player starts to doubt his strategy. He may become afraid to play his hands, and when he does he is not betting them for maximum value. Or, worse yet, he may go on *tilt* and play every hand in hopes of getting his money back.

Definition

Even the best of players are prone to go on **tilt** after a bad beat. To go on tilt is to play poorly due to a loss of emotional control.

The correct strategy is to stay the course, remain focused, and keep concentrating on making correct decisions. Of course, as we will learn later, you have to make adjustments to your opponents. These adjustments will be measured based on the play of your opponents and not on the results of the most recent hands.

Play Within Your Means

Perhaps the most critical factor in helping you make correct decisions is to play within your means. Never play with more money than you can afford to lose. Not only is that irresponsible, it will cause you to make poor decisions.

If you are worried about losing money, you will play scared. You won't bet enough when you should, you'll fold when you shouldn't, and other players will attack you relentlessly. Whenever you sit down to the poker table, you must be willing to risk all of the chips in front of you. If you're not, then find a cheaper game.

Money Is the Name of the Game

In poker you are judged by your results. The objective of poker is to make correct decisions, but the ultimate goal is to win money. It is very easy to keep score. You are either up or down. You are either winning or losing. A common mistake of beginning players is to try to win pots.

Why is that a losing strategy? Think about it this way. If you wanted to win the most pots, you would play every single hand. You'll surely end up winning the most pots, but I guarantee you will lose the most money. That's because while you are playing every hand, your opponents will only be playing their strong hands. You're going to lose a lot more hands than you win even though you will end up winning more hands than anyone else at the table, due to the simple fact that you are playing the most.

What Are You Competing For?

Poker is a competition but it is unlike most competitive endeavors in one important aspect. You are not fighting to win every point. Pick any sport, be it football, baseball, golf, billiards, or darts. Every single down, pitch, shot, or throw, you are going to try your hardest to beat your opponent. In football, if the opposing team runs a trick play such as a flea flicker, the defense has to try its best to stop that play. In poker, if an opponent tries a tricky maneuver to trap you, you're best off just folding and getting out of the way.

If you are a competitive person, when you sit down to the poker table you're going to want to win every hand. You're going to feel personally defeated if you are forced to fold your cards. This is the wrong attitude to have. In poker, you don't have to fight your opponent's best shot. In fact, you shouldn't. Making correct decisions means getting out of the way when your opponent has the *best of it*.

Definition

Having the **best of it** is the best chance of winning the hand at that particular time.

This is not to say that poker isn't competitive, because it is. The trick is that it requires a lot of patience and discipline. You must wait for the right opportunity to jump into the fray and try to win some money. Start thinking in terms of maximizing profits as opposed to winning pots.

Hold 'em

We've all heard Kenny Rogers sing that "you never count your money when you're sitting at the table." That may make for a good song, but it's terrible advice. For reasons we'll learn later, knowing exactly how much money you and each of your opponents has on the table is critical to making correct decisions.

Measure Success Over the Long Term

Your progress in poker should never be based on short-term results. Even the best players will have losing days, weeks, or even months. In order to properly judge your results, you should wait until you have been playing regularly for a few months. During this time, you should be constantly evaluating your play to make sure you are making correct decisions. However, you should not be overly encouraged or discouraged until you have quite a few sessions under your belt.

Try to think of poker as one lifelong game. At the end of that game, you want to come out ahead. There will be some bumps along the way as well as the normal ups and downs, but if you consistently make correct decisions you will make money at the end.

Hold On to Your Chips

First off, let's remember that poker chips are cold hard cash. In addition, that's hard-earned cash on your part. When we are playing with chips instead of money, it's often too easy to forget what those chips represent. Poker is a game, but it is a game played with real money. Chips should not be committed to the pot on a whim. You're playing poker, not gambling needlessly. If you want to gamble, go play slots or roulette.

Once in the Pot, a Chip Is No Longer Yours

Each time it is your turn to act, evaluate each move independently. Don't worry about how much money you have already put in the pot. That money is no longer yours. You have already spent it. Whether you spent it wisely or not is irrelevant.

If you are going to make correct decisions, you must only consider the current action. That doesn't mean you should ignore how much money is in the pot. That is still an important factor in determining pot odds and whether it's worth playing on. Just don't make the mistake of talking yourself into making an expensive call because you have already put too much into the pot already. That's the wrong analysis.

Fold 'em

You'll often hear poker experts exclaim that the player who folds the most, wins the most. That may sound counterintuitive, but good players know to fold hands when they don't have the best of it.

Folding Your Way to Victory

The surest way to conserve chips is to avoid trouble. The surest way to avoid trouble is to fold a lot of hands. Whenever you fold your cards, you know the hand won't cost you any more chips. If you are just getting started or if you haven't played poker in awhile, you are going to want to play some hands.

This is particularly true if you are a recreational player. Whether you are playing for entertainment or for a living, your goal should still be the same. You want to play the right way and become a winning player. We'll cover this topic in much greater detail in Chapter 6, but for now, keep in mind that if you want to win, you are going to have to fold a lot of hands. That may sound boring if you're playing for fun, but ask yourself one question: do you think you'll have more fun if you win or lose?

To use an extreme example, say you fold 2-7, which is a horrible starting hand, and the flop brings 2-2-7. You can't second-guess yourself. Just chuckle to yourself and take comfort in having made the right decision. If you get at all frustrated, you will be sure to start making bad decisions.

Don't Try to Get Back to Even

Remember when we said that you should look at poker as one lifelong game? Keep that in mind next time you find yourself down at the table. Don't feel you have to win everything back. It's okay to have a losing session.

When you are losing, ask yourself if you are playing well and making correct decisions. If so, then continue to play so long as you feel up to it. If you are not playing well, then maybe you should take a break or even leave the table. There will always be another game later on.

Many players make the mistake of either leaving a game too soon when they are ahead or staying in too long when they are behind. Often, if you are ahead, it's because you are playing well and have an edge over your opponents. If that's the case, then you should play as long as you feel up to it. Don't think that you have to quit while you are ahead to ensure you win.

Conversely, if you are losing, be critical in evaluating your play. Often, you are losing because you are being outplayed. If that's the case, you're better off leaving the table and cutting your losses rather than trying to win your money back.

By Any Means Necessary

Poker is a game of deception. Deception is not only accepted but expected. When you sit down at the table, there are nine other players trying to take your money and you are trying to take theirs. We talk about making correct decisions, but keep in mind the context of those decisions.

You are trying to outwit, outplay, and outgun nine other players. At times, you will need to be patient and disciplined. At other times, you will need to be daring and cunning. At all times, you will need to be focused in order to know what mode you should be operating in.

You never know when an opportunity will present itself, so you must be prepared to use any trick in your arsenal at any time. If you lose focus and are not prepared to act, then you will miss an opportunity. When you miss an opportunity, you have not made the correct decision and your play suffers as a result.

A Purpose to Every Action

Every time it is your turn to act, there should be a purpose and a rationale behind your action. Every check, bet, raise, or fold should be made after careful consideration of what is the correct thing to do. In the subsequent chapters, we're going to provide the foundation for you to make the correct decision when it is your turn to act.

For now, remember that every action on your part requires a decision that should never be taken lightly no matter how insignificant it seems at the time. Your poker success depends on you making the correct decision over and over. If that seems like a tall task, it is.

The good thing is you are allowed to make mistakes. Poker is a game of incomplete information, so it's impossible to play perfectly. There is no need to beat yourself up over bad decisions. We all make them. A good player learns from his or her mistakes and moves on.

Texas Hold 'em Basics

Texas Hold 'em (or just plain Hold 'em) is poker's hottest game, and it can be played either as a limit game or a no-limit game. Hold 'em is a seven-card flop game represented by two cards unique to each player and five community cards that are shared by everyone. Each player then makes his best five-card hand. To begin, each player is dealt two cards face down. These are the player's hole cards (or down cards) and can only by seen by the player holding the cards. The cards are dealt clockwise beginning with the player to the dealer's immediate left. The dealer is represented by a small white disc called the button. With each passing hand, the button is passed to the player to the left.

The first player to the left of the button is called the small blind. The second player to the left of the button is called the big blind. Together, they are called the blinds. The players in the blinds must post bets before the cards are dealt. The big blind must put in one full bet and the small blind typically puts in one-half of a full bet.

For instance, in a $5–$10 no-limit Hold 'em game, a full bet for the first round is $10. The big blind posts the $10 bet and the small blind must post a half bet of $5. Since the blinds have already posted their bets, the action begins with the player to the immediate left of the big blind once the cards have been dealt. This player now has the option of calling (matching the full bet amount of the big blind), raising, or folding. In no-limit play, the player can raise any amount from $20 to his entire stack. This first player to act is referred to as being under the gun, since he must make a decision before knowing what any other player may do.

The Gutshot Straight

One of the most critical factors experienced players consider in choosing which hands to play is their position at the table. In a 10-handed game, the two players to the left of the blinds are in early position. The next three players are in middle position and the last three players are in late position. It is preferable to be in late position as you have the advantage of witnessing what others do before it is your turn to act.

After the first player acts, the action then continues clockwise around the table. Each player has the option of calling, raising, or folding. In no-limit, just as the name suggests, there is no limit to the amount of raises or how much one can raise.

When the action gets to the blinds, they have a couple of choices. The small blind is already in for a one-half bet so if no one has raised, the small blind only has to put in another one-half bet in order to call. Of course, the small blind can raise or fold as well. Depending on what has transpired before the action gets to the big blind, he has a couple of choices. First, if no one has raised the big blind, he can *check* since he already has posted a full bet. If he checks, he gets to continue playing without spending any more money. The big blind also has the option of raising. Since the big blind had to post his initial bet without the benefit of seeing his cards, he has the option of raising now that he knows what he's been dealt.

Playing the Flop

Once the first round of betting is complete, the dealer will burn one card (the top card on the deck does not play) and then lay three cards face up in the center of the table. These three cards are turned over simultaneously and collectively are referred to as the *flop*. Everyone at the table can use these community cards. The betting starts anew with the first player to the left of the dealer, who is still in the hand and required to act first. This person can either check or bet. To check means to decline the opportunity to make a bet. You do this by either saying, "Check," or by tapping the table with your hand.

If you check it does not mean you are out of the hand. Do not throw your cards away when you check. Even if you do not like your cards, hold on to them until everyone has had a chance to act. If everyone still in the hand checks as well, then you will get to see the next card for free. That is, you will not have to post any more money. However, once you check the action will move to the next person going clockwise. That person will now have the same opportunity to check or bet. But as soon as anybody bets, the players who act after the bettor cannot check—they must either fold, call, or raise.

Those players who checked before the bettor will also be required to either fold, call, or raise as the action will now continue around. Before we get to the next card, everyone still in the hand must have put in an equal amount of money (the sole exception being when someone is *all-in*, meaning that player has all of her chips in the pot; she is only eligible to win that portion of the pot which matches her contribution).

Definition

The **flop** consists of the first three community cards, which are all dealt at the same time.

When a player declares that she is **all-in**, that means she is betting all of the chips she has on the table. A player can physically put all of her chips in the pot or just state "all-in" to accomplish the same thing.

Here Comes the Turn

Once this second round of betting is over, the dealer will now burn another card before turning over one more community card face up adjacent to the flop cards. This card is called the *turn* card. Each player now has six cards from which to make his or her best five-card hand. The betting proceeds exactly as in the second round.

Down to the River

After the third round of betting is complete, the dealer will burn one more card and turn over one last community card. This card is called the *river*. Now everyone has seven cards (the five shared community cards and each player's unique two hole cards) from which to make his or her best five-card hand. Players can use any five-card combination of these seven cards to make a hand. The betting sequence is exactly the same as rounds two and three.

Finally, a Showdown

Now, after this round of betting is complete, we come to the *showdown*. Each player remaining in the hand will reveal his or her cards and the best hand will win all of the money in the pot. If at any point before the showdown, one player makes a bet or raise and no one else calls, then that player wins the pot without a showdown. This can happen in any round of betting from before the flop to the river.

Hand Rankings

Even though Hold 'em is a seven-card game, players may only use their five best cards. Here are the hand rankings, starting with the best:

Name	Example
Royal flush	Ac Kc Qc Jc Tc
Straight flush	7s 6s 5s 4s 3s
Four of a kind	2222 J
Full house	QQQ 44
Flush	Kh Qh 8h 5h 2h
Straight	98765
Three of a kind	555 Q J
Two pair	KK 77 A
One pair	QQ A 6 5
No pair	K J 8 6 2

The Least You Need to Know

- Poker is a game of skill in the long run so concentrate on making correct decisions instead of short-term profits.
- Play within your means; otherwise you will be playing scared and making bad decisions.
- Think in terms of maximizing profits instead of winning pots.
- Don't squander chips needlessly, because a chip not played is a chip earned.

Techniques to Bluffing

In This Chapter

- Tell a consistent story
- Don't be afraid to get caught
- You can't bluff a sucker
- Sometimes nothing makes a pretty good hand
- The bluff of the century

Bluffing is a powerful tool in poker. To be most effective, it should be employed sparingly and with great discretion. If overused, it will prove disastrous and cost you a lot of money. If underutilized, you will miss out on some great opportunities to win some chips. When used correctly to scoop a big pot when you hold nothing but *rags*, there's no better feeling in all of poker.

Definition

When a player says she has **rags,** she means she has two worthless cards that are unlikely to win against just about any other hand.

Sell Your Hand

The number-one key to a successful bluff is having your opponents believe you. Bluff too frequently and other players will be cynical. They will want to call you. Even if you rarely bluff at all, when you do you will have to sell your hand.

If you are focusing on all the things that you are supposed to at the poker table, you will be studying each one of your opponents. You will notice their mannerisms and expressions and, most important, you will be following their betting patterns. After some time at the table, you will begin to pick up what types of hands they like to play depending on their position. Additionally, you should know which opponents will keep betting strong with starting hands that don't improve, and which players will give up. As you pick up on these tendencies, you will be able to narrow in on what hand your opponent is likely holding.

Now, if your opponents are doing their homework, they'll be studying you just as closely as you are studying them. They will know your tendencies and betting patterns. Don't be alarmed by that. In fact, when it comes to bluffing, that's a good thing. You don't want to bluff an opponent who's not paying attention. You want to bluff the player who is watching your every move.

So how do you get an opponent to believe you? Every hand of poker played tells a story. As the betting progresses and exposed cards are dealt, pieces of the puzzle begin to come together. When you actually have a strong hand, you will play it a certain way. You will, in all likelihood, bet it strong the entire way or you will slow play it in the hopes of trapping an opponent. When you slow play, you are hoping your opponent bets into you and if he does, you spring a big raise on him at the end.

An astute opponent will know when you have a strong hand based on your betting patterns and what cards are on the board. You want to emulate that pattern when you are bluffing. As the hand develops, you want to think about how you would play it if you really had a strong hand.

For instance, say you are in late position and you call an early position raiser with 9d10d because you believe you can outplay your opponent after the flop. The flop comes 3h4hJs. This flop completely missed you but you don't think it helped your opponent, either. Your opponent bets, which you think he would even if he missed the flop. Now, you decide that you are going to play this hand like you have the nine and ten of hearts instead of diamonds. Since you now have a flush draw, you decide to call. The turn is the 6s. This time, it's checked to you. You decide to check and take a *free card*, which is consistent with what you would do if you really had two hearts. The river brings the Kh and your opponent bets. You believe she has a hand like AK and just hit top pair. However, that third heart made your imaginary flush so you make a substantial raise. Your opponent is going to have to give you credit for a flush here. Unless she has a flush herself, she is going to have a hard time calling. Your play throughout the hand was consistent with making a flush.

Definition_____

If the action gets checked around during any betting round with more cards to come, then everyone in the hand gets a **free card**, since it doesn't cost them any money to see this card.

When you don't tell a consistent story, you send mixed signals to your opponents. They have a tougher time comprehending what hand you might hold. When your opponents are confused, they are more likely to be cynical and more likely to call you. Players want to believe that they made the right decision in folding. If they have doubts, then they are going to be naturally curious and more inclined to call you.

Hold 'em

You will have a greater chance of making a successful bluff if you are only up against one opponent as opposed to multiple opponents. That doesn't mean you should never try a bluff against a number of opponents, but keep in mind that it is a lot easier to get one person to fold than three or four.

Show Some Guts

Making a bluff takes guts. You're risking money knowing that if you get called, you are going to lose. Hopefully, by the time you are done reading this chapter, you will realize that a well-timed bluff is not nearly as risky as originally thought.

There's another reason, however, that makes inexperienced players hesitant to bluff. They are embarrassed to get caught. To these players, I have one thing to say—"Get over it!" Actually, I have more to say in the hopes of convincing you. Bluffing is an integral part of the game. If you are going to play the game, you have to implement this aspect into your play. Once you do, you are going to get caught sometimes. In fact, if you never get caught bluffing, you probably aren't bluffing enough. Your opponents don't believe you are capable of a bluff if they never call you on it. And if that's the case, then you probably are not going to make as much money as you should on your strong hands.

Catch Me Now, Pay Me Later

There is a tactical advantage to being caught bluffing. If you are called on the river, you will have to show your cards. When you turn your cards over, the entire table sees your failed bluff attempt. Everyone now knows that you are capable of betting with absolutely nothing. Now, they are more likely to call your bets, including when you have strong hands.

In poker, you are going to make the most money when you get action on your strong hands. In the long run, if you want to be a winning poker player, you have to maximize your winnings on those strong hands. If you only bet your strong hands, you will not make the money you should on these hands. More important, if your *opponents* perceive that you only bet your strong hands, you won't make the money you should.

So if you are making the occasional bluff and not getting called, your opponents still believe that you are only betting your winning hands. Increase your bluffs and don't be afraid to get caught. It will pay off later.

Fold 'em

Avoid trying bluffs when you have a medium-strength hand. If you believe you may have the best hand, then you can win the pot without a bluff attempt. If you do try a bluff, you are only likely to be called by a better hand.

When Is a Bluff Not a Bluff?

When you're bluffing, you are trying to force the better hand to fold. You know you don't have the best hand but you believe your opponent's hand is vulnerable enough that there is a decent chance he will fold to your bet. As simple as this sounds, beginning players often get confused as to what constitutes a bluff. Let's look at an example.

An inexperienced player leads out the betting and continues to bet throughout the hand. The final board reads Kd8d2s9c10d. There was one opponent who had called throughout the hand. Now, on the river the inexperienced player makes a huge bet. His opponent folds and the inexperienced player turns over his KsQs. He states that he made such a big bet on the river because it was a dangerous board in that there were a lot of hands his opponent could have that could beat him.

He was right in that that final card, the 10d, was a dangerous card. It could have made a straight or a flush for his opponent. That's exactly why he should not have made a big bet on the river. If his opponent made a strong hand, he was going to call or raise. You can't bluff an opponent out at that point. The inexperienced player had a strong hand that became very vulnerable by the end. He would have been better served making a small bet at the end. That way, he would have been more likely to get called by a hand that he had beat, such as K-J.

Suckers Don't Fold

There is an old saying in poker that you can't bluff a sucker. Good players will make tough *laydowns* while weak players never will. Inexperienced players spot a poor player at the table and immediately believe that they can bluff him. That's the wrong target. Suckers will lose a lot of money because they will call a lot of bets with losing hands. Since they are calling a lot, they will occasionally catch a player bluffing. This will only encourage their poor play. Attack the poor player when you have good hands, but don't try to bluff them.

Definition

To fold a hand in the face of a bet is called a **laydown**. The better the hand, the tougher it is to lay it down.

Who Can You Bluff?

You can bluff good players who are paying attention to the action at the table. Look for players who will fold hands when they know they are beat. More important, find those players who are playing their opponents and not just their cards. Opponents who are observant and adjust their play depending on who they are up against are the ones you want to try and bluff. Players who blindly play their cards are not who you want to bluff. These players are only interested in the cards that they have and are not paying much attention to their opponents.

Give Players a Reason to Fold

Remember in the previous chapter, we discussed how good players will fold a lot of hands and save their chips. Good players look for a reason to fold. They are not after action; they are looking to win money. They would rather save their chips for a better opportunity.

The Gutshot Straight

It is much harder to call a big bet than it is to make a big bet. David Sklanksy, one of the preeminent poker authors in the world, coined this disparity the Gap Concept. According to Sklansky, there is a significant gap in the strength of your hand needed to call a big raise than the strength of your hand needed to make a big bet in the same situation.

Folding Is the Only Option

There will be times that you bluff, your opponent is fairly certain that you are bluffing and he will fold anyway. Why would he do that? If he doesn't have much of a hand he really doesn't have a lot of choice. In the face of a big bet, folding is the only option unless you know with a great degree of certainty that you have the best hand. If you have a mediocre hand or a *drawing hand*, it simply won't be worth calling a big bet when your sole chance of winning is if your opponent is bluffing.

Definition

A **drawing hand** is hand that has potential but needs help to improve to a winning hand.

Position Is Your Friend

Poker is a positional game. There is a huge advantage in being able to decide what to do after having the opportunity to witness your opponents' actions. In Hold 'em, when you are in late position, you will maintain that position for each betting round. You want to play more hands from late position than any other and you will have the most opportunities to bluff from that position.

No Fold 'em Hold 'em

In many low-stakes games, bluffing is just not going to work. These games are populated with amateurs and tourists who want to play a lot of hands. They are more interested in being entertained than making money. More importantly, they do not understand the importance of a good laydown.

More experienced players derisively refer to these games as no fold 'em Hold 'em. No matter what cards you have or how much money you bet, someone is going to call you. These games can be very profitable for you as you are likely to make a lot of money with your good hands. Keep in mind two things when playing these games. First, bluffing will rarely work. Next, you will lose a lot of hands against opponents who suck out on you at the end. Instead of getting frustrated at this, take comfort in the fact that your opponents are playing poorly and will pay you off eventually.

While the no fold 'em Hold 'em tables are primarily found at the lower limits, you will still find some players who fit this description in some more expensive games.

Bluffin' with Nothin'

It's hard to make a big bet or raise when you hold a lousy hand. Everyone likes the security blanket of having good cards. Of course, I'd much rather be all-in with the nuts than rags. However, if you are only willing to bet with the nuts, you are never going to be a winning poker player. If you are not used to bluffing, there is a big mental hurdle to get over. I'm going to give you a couple of tips to help you leap that hurdle.

The Gutshot Straight

According to poker legend, the term *the nuts* dates back to card playing in the Old West. When a player was out of cash and wanted to bet his horse and wagon, he was required to take the nut bolts off the wheels of his wagon and place them in the pot. This would prohibit the player from trying to escape if he lost. Since a player would be stranded if he lost the pot, he would be crazy to bet the nuts with anything less than the best possible hand.

Ignore Your Cards

The point of bluffing is that you want your opponents to fold. If you are successful, it doesn't matter if you hold pocket Aces or 2-7 offsuit. No one will ever see your cards. Try to pick a situation ahead of time to attempt a bluff under favorable conditions.

Next time you play, tell yourself that you are going to bluff the second time that everyone folds to you in the *cutoff* position. Observant players will note that you did not raise the first time this happened and will be more likely to give you credit for a hand. You now only have to worry about three players behind you (the button, the small blind, and the big blind). Of those three, only the button will have position on you.

Definition

The position to the immediate right of the button is called the **cutoff**. It is so called because the player in that position has the opportunity to raise and force the player on the button to fold. By doing so, the raising player has cut off the button and now enjoys the best position.

Don't look at your cards until it is your turn to act. Now, when everyone folds to you in the cutoff for the second time, you know you are going to raise. Take a look at your cards and pretend that you have pocket Aces and raise accordingly. If you get called, continue to bet or raise after the flop. Don't get discouraged if this doesn't work the first time. If nothing else, it will get you used to betting with nothing and if you get caught, you have set yourself up to get paid with winning hands later.

Give Yourself Two Chances to Win

When you bluff pre-flop, you give yourself two chances to win. First, if you force your opponents to fold, you win the pot uncontested. Next, if you get called, you could still end up making the best hand and win the pot that way. If you never bluff, you are only going to win pots when you have the best hand.

You're Not as Big a Dog as You Think

If you are bluffing pre-flop and get called, you still have a lot of chances to win. Even if your hand doesn't improve, you have an excellent chance to take down the pot so long as your opponent's hand doesn't improve. Since you have taken the lead in being aggressive, your opponents are going to be proceeding cautiously.

You are never that big of an underdog pre-flop. Even if you hold 7-2 offsuit and are up against Aces, you still have a percent chance of winning the hand.

Track Your Play

If you are having trouble pulling the trigger on a bluff, here's a little confidence builder. Next time you play, count how many hands you win without a showdown, and also what percentage of your wins come without a showdown. Since you are not bluffing, all those wins presumably came when you had the best hand.

However, since you won without a showdown, it really didn't matter what cards you had. Those cards just gave you the crutch to bet aggressively. You could have bet the same way and won the hand with absolutely nothing if you only had the confidence to do so. By tracking your play and realizing how many hands you are winning without a showdown, you will hopefully gain that confidence.

A Major Bluff

In 2003, amateur poker player Chris Moneymaker won the main event of the World Series of Poker after qualifying for the event by winning a qualifying tournament at an online site that only cost him $40. His victory, shown over and over on ESPN, is widely credited for helping fuel the current poker craze. The turning point for Moneymaker came on one critical hand that became known as the "Bluff of the Century." While that characterization may be a little premature, Moneymaker's bluff embodied just about every aspect of a successful bluff, so let's take a detailed look at the hand.

At the very end of the tournament, amateur Chris Moneymaker was heads-up with savvy pro Sam Farha. Moneymaker had a slight lead with $4.62 million to Farha's $3.77 million. The blinds were $20,000 to $40,000 with a $5,000 ante. Chris Moneymaker was in the small blind, which was also the button. He had favorable position in that he would act last every round after the flop. Moneymaker was dealt KsJh and decided to raise to $100,000. Farha called from the big blind with Qs9h.

The flop came 9s2d6s, giving Farha top pair. Curiously, Farha checked his top pair. Perhaps he was trying to trap Moneymaker, but a pair of nines is certainly a vulnerable hand. Moneymaker checked as well.

The turn was the 8s. Farha still had top pair and he bet $300,000. Moneymaker now had an open-ended straight draw as well as the second nut flush draw. Moneymaker hesitated for a brief moment before raising another $500,000. This raise certainly represented strength on Moneymaker's part and Farha had to be concerned. With a board of 9s2d6s8s, Moneymaker could easily have a straight, a flush, or two pair—all hands that would beat Farha. Nonetheless, Farha called rather quickly.

The river brought the 3h and did not improve either player's hand. Farha checked this time and Moneymaker quickly declared that he was all-in. Moneymaker had completely missed both his flush and a straight and was bluffing with absolutely nothing but a king high. He was putting it to the ultimate test.

Now, here is where things get interesting. Farha took a very long time to decide whether to call or not. In fact, he even asked out loud at one point, "You must have missed your flush, huh?" Certainly, Farha contemplated that a bluff was a very real possibility. After much deliberation, however, Farha finally folded his hand.

Let's take a look at why this bluff was successful. First, these players had been playing at the final table for over 10 hours. During that time, Moneymaker had rarely bluffed and Farha knew that. More important, Moneymaker knew that Farha had to know that Moneymaker had not bluffed much at all. Next, Moneymaker told a consistent story. He made a substantial raise on the turn, which had to scare Farha. That turn raise set up his all-in bluff on the river. Moneymaker was able to make that raise on the turn due to his favorable position. If Moneymaker did not have position during this hand, arguably he never makes the bluff.

Finally, Moneymaker knew that Farha was capable of making a big laydown. He knew his opponent could be bluffed even if Farha suspected a bluff. When the action came down to those two players heads-up, Moneymaker had approached Farha about making a deal. Even though Moneymaker had the chip lead, he was willing to split the remaining prize money equally, which would have been a favorable proposition to Farha. Farha declined, however, believing that he was the better player and he could outplay Moneymaker.

Since Farha sincerely believed he was the best player, would he be willing to risk his entire tournament life by calling in this situation? From Farha's long deliberation to subsequent interviews he gave on the subject, there is strong evidence that Farha did indeed believe Moneymaker was bluffing. Even so, he still could not risk the world championship on a hunch. Moneymaker knew that Farha thought he was the superior player and thus would rather wait for a more opportune time to play for all of his chips. Moneymaker bluffed a very good player at just the right time when all of the factors for a successful bluff were present.

The Least You Need to Know

- Make your opponents believe you have a strong hand when you bluff so that they will fold and surrender the pot to you.

- Don't worry about getting caught when you bluff because if you do, your opponents may become overly cynical and pay you off when you have a strong hand.

- Try bluffs on strong players who are paying attention and who are capable of folding.

- When you're bluffing, it makes no difference what cards you have because your only chance of winning is to force your opponent to fold.

Chapter 3

Other Forms of Deception

In This Chapter

- Slow playing
- Sticking with a plan
- The semi-bluff
- Create confusion

Poker is a game of deception. Deception embodies more than just bluffing. Hiding the strength of your powerful hands is arguably more profitable than bluffing. Poker is also a game of small edges and many nuances. Being aggressive and deceptive is the best way for players to exploit those edges. In this chapter, we're going to explore some of the ways to deceive that may not be as sexy as bluffing but are just as critical to your overall success.

Pretending to Be Weak

Conceptually, slow playing is the polar opposite of bluffing. When bluffing, your goal is to bet enough to force a superior hand to fold when you know you are beat. When slow playing, you are trying to induce your opponent to stay in the hand when you know you have her beat.

The purpose of the slow play is to hide the strength of your hand. By not betting, you hope that your opponent takes that as a sign of weakness. There are two keys to a successful slow play. First, your opponent must believe your deceptive signal that you do not possess a strong hand. Next, you must have the best hand and your opponent is not likely to draw out on you. Let's examine each of these components.

Selling the Slow Play

Unlike a bluff, a slow play is more likely to work against poor players. Poor players like to play their cards in a vacuum. If they have a hand, they will bet it. And if they don't have anything yet, by slow playing you give them the chance to improve their hand and bet it. Once you induce them to bet, you can go ahead and raise an amount you think they are likely to call.

Good, astute players will be familiar with slow-playing tactics and are likely to tread cautiously. As with everything in poker, there are a couple of exceptions to this generalization. If you have been

playing very conservatively and checking and calling
your marginal hands and your drawing hands, then
a solid astute opponent may believe your slow-play
tactic. Slow playing also works very well against
hyper-aggressive opponents. If you know your
opponent loves to bet at any pot you check, then let
him.

Hold 'em

> You don't want to slow play hands
> when your opponents have a chance
> to outdraw you if you give them a free
> card. Make your opponents pay to get
> those cards.

Make Sure You Have the Best Hand

If you are going to slow play, be sure you have the
best hand. For example, if the flop comes 6-6-5
and you hold a 6-5, then you now have a full house
and the absolute nuts. It's a fairly safe bet that your
hand will hold up as the best through a showdown.
Your goal at this point is to maximize value and,
depending on the nature of your opponents, slow
playing is a viable option.

Let's look at a different situation. You hold pocket
Aces in the small blind and everyone folds to you.
You just call hoping to hide the strength of your
hand as the big blind checks. The flop comes
10s8d2s. This seems like a good flop for you and
you decide to slow play and hope the big blind leads

the way. This is not a good choice. The big blind could have anything in this situation. He could have two pair, a flush draw, or a straight draw.

While he is unlikely to put you on a pair of Kings, you are still better off betting out in this situation. The reason being is that you are more likely to gain information about your opponent's hand by betting. If he calls or raises, you are more likely to believe he has a decent hand than if you check and then allow him the chance to bet. This will help you gauge if in fact you have the best hand.

Setting the Trap

The ultimate example of this is Johnny Chan's play in the final stages of the 1988 World Series of Poker as memorialized in the movie *Rounders*. Johnny Chan was heads-up with Erik Seidel when he flopped the nut straight. Chan held Jc9c and the flop was Qs10d8d. Seidel held a Queen with a weak kicker, giving him top pair. There was $40,000 in the pot and Chan was first to act after the flop. He checked. Seidel bet $50,000, which Chan called. The turn brought a blank and again Chan checked. However, this time Seidel checked, also. The river brought another blank and again Chan checked. This time Seidel went all-in and, of course, Chan called (right away I might add). Seidel was severely crippled and shortly thereafter Chan was world

champion. Chan took a big chance by checking on
the river. If Seidel had checked also, then Chan
would have lost the opportunity to make a bet with
the nuts. However, by checking his last opportunity
to bet, Chan projected weakness that he hoped
Seidel would seek to exploit. Seidel did and Chan
maximized his profit. Certainly if Chan had gone all
in first, Seidel would have folded.

Fold 'em

Don't underestimate the value of *kick-
ers.* When you hold K-10 and the flop
comes K-6-5, don't get married to your
hand. Opponents willing to bet and raise
this flop are likely to have a hand that
dominates you such as A-K, K-Q, or K-J.

Don't Get Too Cute

Say you are holding pocket 3s and you get to see a
flop cheaply from late position after two players in
front of you limp in. The big blind checks and four
of you are in the hand. This is an ideal situation for
you. You are in position and have a hand that plays
well in a multi-way pot and you get to see the flop
cheaply. If you hit a *set* of 3s, you can likely win a
big pot. If you miss, this is an easy hand to get away
from.

> **Definition**
>
> A **set** is a hand that contains three of a kind with two of those cards in your hand. You must have a pocket pair and hit another card of your rank on the board in order to make a set. Compare this with **trips**, which is a hand containing three of a kind with one of those cards in your hand and two on the board.

The flop comes KdJc3c. This is a great flop for you. Not only did you hit your set of 3s, there is a strong likelihood that one or more of your opponents have been helped by this flop and have made either top pair or even two pair. Since no one raised pre-flop, it's unlikely that an opponent is holding pocket Kings or pocket Jacks. Your hand should be the best hand at this point. The key parts of that previous sentence are the words "at this point." There are still two cards to come and there are a lot of potential draws out there. An opponent holding two clubs is drawing to a flush and someone holding a hand like A-Q or Q-10 would be drawing to a straight.

This is not the time to slow play. Bet and raise and make your bets substantial. You should be looking to make pot-sized bets or raises. If you get called, you are building a bigger pot and you are making your opponent pay for the chance to outdraw you. If everyone else folds, so be it. Take the pot and be happy with the chips.

If you don't bet your hand in this situation, then you are allowing your opponent the chance to beat you. If she misses her draw, then she is unlikely to commit any more chips. If she makes her draw, then you are going to lose the hand. The best way to win more money here is to make your opponent pay for the chance to outdraw you.

The Gutshot Straight

Not surprisingly, many of the old-school top poker players hail from Texas. Back in the day, they would travel the state looking for a juicy game. During these days, the starting hand of A-K became known as "walking back to Houston." This nickname came about because of the tendency of players to overplay the hand, lose a lot of money, and end up either literally or figuratively walking back to Houston.

Playing Monsters Pre-Flop

There are two schools of thought to playing monster hands such as A-A, K-K, or even A-K. The first school of thought rationalizes that you only get dealt a limited amount of these hands so when you get them, you need to slow play in order to maximize your profit. You want to give your opponents a chance to get involved in the hand so you get action.

The other school of thought is to play these hands strongly from the get-go and eliminate opponents. The rationale here is that you will either win a small pot or lose a large one, as you will have a hard time folding your Aces if someone else's hand improves.

So which school should you follow? To answer that, let's take a look at the likelihood of success with each hand. With pocket Aces, you know you are going to be a substantial favorite against any other hand—unless an opponent holds the other two Aces, which is so unlikely that it should never enter into your thought process. However, if you are up against five opponents, you are now an underdog against these opponents collectively. The more players in the pot, the less likely you are to win.

Let's look at position, then, in deciding what to do with pocket Aces. From early position, you should just about always raise. You don't want to give too many people the opportunity to enter the pot, especially when you will be out of position throughout the hand. Furthermore, not only do you weed out opponents by raising, you are likely to only get called by hands that you are a big favorite against. Players holding hands like A-K, K-K, or Q-Q are more likely to call than players holding a hand like 10-9 suited. However, of all of those hands, the 10-9 suited has the best chance of beating my Aces.

The only situation in which you should not raise with pocket Aces from early position is if you were playing at a table with one or more very aggressive players who are likely to raise behind you if you just call. In that situation, let them raise and then re-raise when the action gets back to you.

You should only slow play Aces from late position when no one has entered the pot before you. If everyone folds to you in the cutoff or the button, then with only a couple of people to act behind you, you should not be as concerned with allowing too many players to enter the pot. By just calling, you may get one or two opponents in the pot who will give you some action. You may even induce a player to raise pre-flop, in which case you can re-raise him. There is one caveat to this attempted slow play. If you typically always raise from late position when the action is folded to you, it's probably wise then to raise with your pocket Aces. If you don't, an astute player may suspect something. If you do raise, your opponents are likely to believe you are making a positional raise and not give you credit for a strong hand.

Hold 'em

There are no absolutes in poker. The advice contained in this book is meant to give you a solid foundation to build off of. As you gain experience, you should strive to find your own style and make your own judgments that will allow you to play to your fullest potential.

With pocket Kings, I will almost never slow play. From early and middle position, it's important to raise to keep opponents from limping in with a hand like A-8 suited. If you make a substantial raise, you should chase out all the Aces except pocket Aces, A-K, and possibly A-Q. If someone raises before me, I'll re-raise with a pot-size raise with my Kings.

Even in late position, I'll open raise with Kings. My opponents may put me on a positional raise and I do not want to afford them the opportunity to see a flop with a weak Ace.

Holding A-K is a whole different animal. A-K can be a powerful hand, yet it is an underdog to any-one holding a pocket pair. Granted, it's only a very slight underdog to a pair of Queens or below. In addition, A-K dominates any weaker Ace such as these playable hands: A-Q, A-J, or A-10. I tend to open raise with A-K from any position. However, if someone has raised before me, I will typically just call and I may even fold. For instance, if there is a raise and a re-raise from a tight player, I'll fold A-K. Facing one standard raise of three times the big blind, I will generally call and wait to see what the flop brings.

The only time I will consider slow playing A-K is if I am in late position and there have been one or two limpers in front of me. In this case, I may call, hoping to hit a flop and win a big pot.

Fire Multiple Bullets

There's an old expression that an amateur will only fire one bullet while a seasoned pro will fire two, three, or even four. What this means is that an amateur will raise before the flop and then check or fold if her hand does not improve on the flop. A top player won't give up on the hand and will continue to bet the flop, turn, and possibly river in order to win the hand.

Don't give up on a hand too quickly. Even if the flop doesn't help you, there's only a 1–3 chance that it helped your opponent if he did not have a pocket pair to start. If your opponent did have a pocket pair, then cards that are higher than his pair on the board will have to worry him.

Let's look at a specific example. Say you raise with AhQh in early position and only the player on the button calls you. You know this player likes to play a lot of hands from late position. The flop comes Ks9h2c. This does not help you at all. However, unless your opponent is holding pocket 9s, pocket 2s, or a King, he is not going to like this flop, either. Even if he has a King, he may be worried that he is outkicked.

More important, your opponent is likely to believe this flop helped you since a hand like A-K is one you would raise with from early position. This is a perfect opportunity to keep firing bullets.

Certainly, there will be times when you will need to put on the brakes and give up a hand when it doesn't improve—especially in multi-way pots. Examine your own play. If you are never firing bullets when you miss the flop—especially when you are heads-up—you are forfeiting too many pots.

Playing with Outs

A distant cousin to the bluff play is the semi-bluff. A semi-bluff differs greatly from the bluff in that you may still have a chance to win if you are called. When you bluff, you have a weak hand and you know the only chance to win is to force your opponent to fold.

With a semi-bluff, you hope to force your opponent to fold and win the hand right there. However, if your opponent does call, you still have a draw to the best hand. For example, say the board reads As8h9c2s after the turn. You are holding Js10s, giving you both an open-ended straight draw and a flush draw. Of course, right now you don't have anything. There are a lot of cards that can make a winning hand for you on the river. You also think your opponent has an Ace with a weak kicker, so he's vulnerable. This is a great opportunity to implement a semi-bluff.

A semi-bluff only works when there are more cards to come that could make you the best hand. A semi-bluff is not a bet when you have a marginal hand and you hope to force your opponent out, but if you don't you think your hand as exists may still win. That is not a semi-bluff or a bluff. That's a poor play. If you have a mediocre hand that you think might win, then the correct move is to check or call.

Keep Them Guessing

If you recall, in the last chapter, we discussed the importance of telling a consistent story when attempting a bluff. In order to sell that bluff, you want your opponents to believe you have a strong hand. When you actually have a strong hand, you want action. If your opponents are cynical, then they are more likely to call.

By creating confusion, you arouse a natural state of curiosity in your opponent's mind. Curiosity compels players to stay in and find out what you have. There are a number of ways to create confusion and keep your opponents off balance.

Aggression Pays Off

Constant aggression keeps maximum pressure on opponents. Many successful players are very adept at this style. They play a lot of hands, and when they play they are betting and raising. By doing this, it becomes very difficult for opponents to know what kind of hand the aggressive player has.

Consistent aggression actually causes confusion. Even though opponents will expect the aggressive play, they will intuitively know that the aggressor cannot always have good hands. Opponents then tend to wait for strong hands in the hopes of trapping the aggressor. A solid aggressive player, though, will be very wary of traps and will be adept at folding hands when he is beat.

This is not a style that is easy to pull off and I don't recommend it for everybody. I would suggest, however, that you experiment with it to see how effective it can be and to understand the mindset of this common and effective opponent.

Don't Be Predictable

Studying your opponents and knowing their betting habits and tendencies is a critical component to maximizing your play and your profits at the table. Of course, we have to remember that our opponents (at least the good ones) are studying us as much as we are studying them.

Thus, it becomes important for us to not be too predictable. We shouldn't always do the same thing in the same situation. If everyone folds to us on the button, we shouldn't raise every time. We should call at times and even fold occasionally. We should slow play monster hands at times and play them fast at others. We should mix in bluffs and not be afraid to get caught. We should occasionally implement semi-bluffs with drawing hands and just call or check at other times. All of these are good strategies for just about any game.

If you play in a regular game with the same opponents, you can take this concept even further. For instance, while I would just about always raise with pocket Aces in early position, I will mix in an occasional call with that hand to keep my opponents guessing. Since I play in a biweekly game, I will get Aces in early position enough times to make this play worthwhile. If you sit down in a casino to play for two hours with players coming and going, these subtle plays won't be worth it since they are unlikely to occur enough to be relevant.

The Least You Need to Know

- Deceptive play is a lot more than just bluffing, as hiding the strength of your hand can prove just as valuable as bluffing with a weak hand.

- Slow playing can help you maximize profits by tricking your opponents to bet into your strong hands.

- Semi-bluffing can be a valuable tool in that you can win a pot either by forcing your opponents to fold or by making your draw.

- Mix up your play to keep your opponents off balance.

Chapter

Measuring Risk vs. Reward

In This Chapter

- Know your opponents
- Don't bet a lot to win a little
- Play poker, don't gamble

Playing is an extremely nuanced game and a game of small edges. In this chapter, we'll try to help you identify and exploit those edges. Poker is a game of imperfect information. Developing skills to help you gain as much information as possible will help you take measured risks when you perceive an advantage.

Reading the Competition

In the long run, everyone will get their fair share of good hands. If every player won the hand when she had the best one, then you're not playing poker. You might as well turn the cards up and let the chips fall where they fall. Of course, poker is not played that way. (If your game is played that way, you will clean up after reading this book.)

There are a lot of ways to give yourself an advantage that goes beyond the cards you are dealt. The number-one way is knowing your opponents. How do you accomplish that? By maintaining your focus and carefully studying your opponents. If you are playing in a 10-handed game, you will not be playing in the great majority of hands. But stay involved in those hands. Don't doze off or watch the game on the television across the room. Watch your opponents and try to guess what hands they have. Within a short period of time, I think you will be amazed at how accurately you can guess.

This newfound knowledge will be gained from observing betting patterns and tendencies more than tells. Tells are important (and beyond the scope of this book), but they are rarely as obvious as on television. In addition, even when you pick up on a tell, you may not find it as useful as betting patterns and tendencies.

As a starting point, you should try to answer the following questions about as many players as possible:

- What hands will she raise with?
- What hands will she call with?
- Will she play passively or aggressively?
- Will she ever slow play hands?
- Will she ever bluff?
- How much attention does she pay to her opponents?

Once you answer these questions, see if you can place each player into the following categories. Keep in mind that these are just generalizations and more accomplished players will be adept at mixing up their play and won't be so easily characterized. Most beginning to intermediate players will however, and they will be fairly consistent.

Don't try to do too much at once. If you're just starting out, concentrate on one player until you get the hang of this.

The Calling Station

The *calling station* is a loose, passive player and is the ideal opponent. He will play a lot of hands and rarely take the lead in betting or raising. He doesn't consider things like pot odds or what cards his opponents might hold. Many novices and recreational players fall into this category. They view poker as more of a gamble than a skill. The calling station fails to recognize the many and varied subtleties of the game.

If you find a calling station at your table, try to isolate him pre-flop any time you have a decent hand. You don't need a great hand to play against him since he will be playing just about anything. So long as your hand remains strong, keep betting into him. Calling stations will often fold on the river when they miss their draws, so don't shy away from firing bullets at them even if your hand fails to improve. Since the calling station is notorious for calling, the only time you should bluff is when you believe he has missed his draw on the river. If the calling station ever raises, then warning signals should go off. Unless you have a strong hand, you should probably fold.

Definition

The ideal opponent is the **calling station.** The calling station is a player who will call a lot of bets but will rarely bet or raise himself. Don't try bluffing these players but let them pay off your winning hands.

The Maniac

The maniac is a loose, aggressive player who likes a lot of action. She will play a lot of hands and when she does, she will bet and raise at every opportunity.

Her philosophy is to put maximum pressure on her opponents.

There are really two different types of maniacs. First is the clueless maniac who has no real sense of purpose to her betting patterns other than having fun and splashing chips around. Against this player, you want to play more hands than you normally would so long as you are heads-up against her. If you can isolate the clueless maniac with above-average hands, you will win a lot of money in the long run—although be prepared for some expensive hits (bad beats) along the way.

The Gutshot Straight

It's considered bad etiquette to complain about a bad beat. We all suffer from them from time to time and if you play long enough, you'll endure your fair share. So it's best to keep the bad beat stories to yourself. You'll feel better and you won't look like a novice to the other players.

Since each hand the maniac plays will be expensive, many of the other players will only be willing to play their strongest hands. When others enter the pot, then only play your strongest hands. Trying to bluff a clueless maniac is rarely worth it.

The second type of maniac is the skilled maniac. These players appear to be out of control but there is actually a method to their madness. The skilled maniac will exert maximum pressure on her opponents and scoop every loose pot that no one else is willing to take. She is a master at hiding the value of her hands since she is playing every hand aggressively. When she does hit a strong hand, her opponents are unlikely to believe her and she can win some big pots.

Fold 'em

If you find yourself at a table with two or more maniacs, the game may be more expensive than you bargained for. Don't stay in a game when the stakes take you out of your comfort zone. Find a game better suited for you so you can play to the best of your ability.

Against the skilled maniac you have to be more selective. You can wait for only very strong hands and then hope to trap her and win a big pot. That is certainly a viable option. However, what separates the skilled maniac from the clueless maniac is her ability to avoid trouble. This creates another opportunity for you. You can bluff the skilled maniac and, in fact, you should bluff her more than you would most other opponents.

The skilled maniac knows that astute opponents will try to trap her, so the best way to bluff her is by pretending to set a trap. For example, say the skilled maniac is in late position and you know she routinely raises from this spot unless there are one or two big raises before the action gets to her. So everyone folds to you in middle position. You limp in with 4-7 offsuit, which is not a hand worth playing. Sure enough, our maniac raises. Everyone folds around to you. Now, you re-raise. Don't be surprised if the maniac calls instead of folding. You can still win the hand. No matter what the flop brings, check raise the maniac. Now, she is sure to believe you and will fold all but her strongest hands.

Combing an occasional bluff along with playing your strong hands against the skilled maniac will serve a larger purpose. The skilled maniac is not looking for action. She is looking to make money. Once she recognizes you as a formidable opponent, she is likely to slow down against you and target others at the table who are more likely to roll over.

The Rock

The rock is a tight, aggressive player. This is where you will categorize the more experienced solid players. In fact, most of the poker literature describes this type of play as most optimal. Certainly, adopting this style can be profitable, especially when up against less experienced opposition.

The rock will only enter pots when he has a strong hand, but when he does, he will come out swinging. He will bet and raise. Even if he misses the flop, he is likely to continue his aggressive ways unless someone plays back at him. For instance, say the rock raises from early position with AsKs and gets one caller. The flop comes Qd9c2d. The rock is likely to keep betting in the hopes of cashing in on his reputation.

The rock knows that his more astute opponents will recognize him as a tight and aggressive player and are likely to give him credit for a strong hand when he enters a pot. The rock will also use his reputation to make a well-timed bluff.

Avoid going up against a rock with marginal or trouble hands. If he open raises from early position, then you don't want to play hands like A-J or A-10. You could lose a lot of money to a hand like A-A, A-K, or A-Q. And if you do end up with the best hand, the rock is unlikely to pay you off.

You can bluff a rock, especially if you have position. For instance, say the rock open raises from middle position and you call from the button with 6d7d. The flop comes 2c5d9h. The rock continues to bet even though you don't think this flop helped him. The rock is not one to give up easily on a pot once he enters, so rather than raise him here, just call. If you raise, he may suspect you are trying to steal. By calling, you actually may signal a stronger hand. Now, when the turn comes, if the rock does not improve, there is fairly good chance he will check. When he does, bet out big and force him to fold.

The Slow Bleeder

The slow bleeder is a tight, passive player. Just like the rock, she will only play her strongest hands. Unlike the rock, when she does play, she is likely to just call and if she doesn't improve, she will get out of the hand. This will keep her from losing a lot of money in a hurry, but she will lose money slowly and surely.

All those times she enters the pot and doesn't improve will cost her money. In addition, since she's not raising, she's inviting a lot of players into the pot to play against her, greatly reducing her chance of winning. Finally, when she does have a strong hand, her opponents will know it and get out of her way.

When up against the slow bleeder, stay on the offensive. Try to see flops with her and then attack. If she is vulnerable, she will fold. If she calls, make a determination as to whether she is on a draw or has a hand. If on a draw, then keep attacking after the turn.

 Hold 'em

Experiment with a number of different styles. That will allow you to find what works for you as well as allow you to seamlessly change styles depending on the situation.

Find Your Optimal Strategy

Now that we know what types of opponents you are likely to encounter and how to identify them, take a moment to examine your own play. How would you characterize yourself? If you are a calling station, a clueless maniac, or a slow bleeder, then you have a lot of work to do. If you are a skilled maniac or a rock, then you are on the right track.

Assuming you are reading this book because you want to improve, I would suggest that you begin by trying to adopt the philosophy of the rock. From there, we can make adjustments. Try to look at it this way. Playing like a rock is playing by the book. You are playing fundamentally solid poker. Like most disciplines in life, playing by the book will only get you so far. However, you need to know the fundamentals before learning how to deviate from them.

Playing like a skilled maniac is an extremely difficult style to pull off and is not going to be right for most players. The skilled maniac will be profitable in the long run, but she will also have a much greater variance in her bankroll than the rock will. Since the nature of poker will cause large short-term swings anyway, few can stomach the added exposure that playing like a maniac will bring.

I would suggest that you test the waters of playing like a maniac by trying it out on occasion against some slow bleeders. Find a level of comfort that you can adopt to your overall game. Once you have that level of comfort, you will find yourself with the ability to switch gears seamlessly as the situation dictates. In poker, you should sit down to the table with an open mind. Don't have a preconceived notion of how you should play. Rather, be willing to adapt to your opponents and the situation at hand.

Finally, be aware that your opponents will be trying to categorize your play just as you are trying to identify them. Make it difficult for them by being unpredictable.

Be Smart with Your Bets

No matter what the purpose of your bet or raise, don't risk a lot to win a little. Keep the size of your bet in perspective. If there's $60 in the pot, then betting $300 doesn't make a lot of sense. If you have the strongest hand, you are unlikely to get called. If you are bluffing, there's no need to risk that much.

The Gutshot Straight

When you are out of chips and nothing stands between you and the top of the table, you are down to the felt or felted.

A Big Bet May Send the Wrong Signal

When bluffing, you don't want your bet to look suspicious. Your goal is to make your opponents believe you. If you really had a strong hand, how much would you bet? That should be your starting point and you can adjust up a little if you think you need to for the particular opponent you are up against.

A Smaller Bet May Do the Same Job ... and Better

When there's not a lot of money in the pot, a small bet will usually chase out opponents who don't have much of a hand. They don't want to get sucked into a pot that's not worth chasing. If you make an overly big pot, you not only arouse suspicion, you now invite others to take advantage of you. If a player has a good hand and is slow playing, he's going to call or raise you whether you make the small or large bet, so there's no need to make the large bet. However, the player who would have folded to a small bet may now find the pot large enough to make a play for. Your big bet increases the pot so it becomes more enticing for an opponent to raise.

Give Skill a Chance

If you want to gamble, go play slots or roulette. At least then you can know the house has an edge. If you are not playing smart poker, you are giving your opponents an enormous edge. Don't call big bets looking for that miracle card.

Presumably, you play poker because you believe you are better than your opponents. You're reading up on the game and developing your skills. You're trying to make correct decisions. That's all great. Now, remember to be patient.

Don't force the action. Poker can be a very streaky game. There will be times when the cards will run bad for you. If you haven't seen anything better than J-3 for a couple of rounds of play, don't be tempted to play Q-8 offsuit out of position.

Wait until you have decent cards or you sense your opponents are vulnerable and you can capitalize on the fact that you haven't played a hand in quite some time. Your time will come if you hang in there. Resist the temptation to gamble and play smart poker no matter what the situation.

The Gutshot Straight

Many players only half-jokingly refer to A-Q as the worst starting hand in no-limit Texas Hold 'em. The reason is that it's the hand that can cost you a lot of money when you are up against a superior hand such as A-K, and you are unlikely to win a lot of money with it against a weaker Ace.

Don't Risk It All on a Small Edge

If you believe you are better than your opponents, then don't get caught in the trap of playing huge pots with a slight edge. For instance, say the blinds are $1 and $2 and you sit down to the table with $200, which represents your entire bankroll. You are in the big blind and everyone folds to the small blind. The small blind inadvertently flashes you his cards, which are the AsKs. He then moves all-in for

$200. You have two red 4s in your hand, making you about a 51 percent favorite to win the hand. Do you really want to risk your entire bankroll on such a tiny advantage? If you have the skill, you're going to find much better opportunities to get your money in the pot.

The Least You Need to Know

- Identify the playing style of your opponents.
- Adjust your play to the style of your opponents.
- Know what kind of player you are and keep your opponents guessing.
- Don't risk a lot to win a little.

Value Betting

In This Chapter

- Getting paid
- Don't fall in love
- The price of poker
- The texture of the game

Playing winning poker is not about winning pots. It's about winning money. It's better to win a few select pots rather than play a lot of hands in the hopes of winning more. More important, when you have a strong hand you want to extract as much money as possible from your opponents. The skill to accomplish that is perhaps the most important skill to becoming a successful player. In this chapter, we are going to help you develop and hone that skill.

Give Action to Get Action

If the idea is to win money, not pots, then it makes sense to only play the strongest hands, right? After all, those hands are the ones that are likely to hold up and take down the pot for you. This strategy sounds good in theory but will rarely work in reality.

If you were playing against an opponent who only played very strong hands, what would you do when she entered a pot? You would (or you should, anyway) fold everything but the very strongest hands. That's what your opponents are going to do if you only play the nuts.

In order to maximize your winnings when you have a strong hand, you need to play other hands as well. Play some drawing hands and use position to play more marginal holdings. For instance, call a small raise with a hand like 8s7s and if everyone folds to you on the button, raise with a hand like 9-7 offsuit.

Playing these hands in these situations accomplishes a couple of things for you. First, if you hit the flop, you could win a sizeable pot as the value of your hand will be well hidden. Next, even if you don't win with these hands, you signal to your opponents that you are willing to play more than just super strong hands. Just don't get carried away with these hands, and be prepared to fold if you miss the flop and an opponent leads out betting. When you do get a monster, your opponents are more likely to give you action.

Hold 'em

No-limit is played for table stakes. A player can only bet or call that amount of chips or money that she has in front of her on the table. If you have $100 left and your opponent bets $200, you can still call but you can only win $100 from your opponent. If another opponent then calls the $200 bet, then you can win $100 from each of them but the extra $200 goes into a side pot that only one of your opponents can win.

Bet to Win Money

When you have a strong hand, the goal becomes one of maximizing profit. For instance, say you have two Jacks and the flop comes J-6-2 *rainbow* (with one spade). You have the very best possible hand right now. More important, it is unlikely that an opponent will have a drawing hand to a flush or a straight with this board.

Definition

A **rainbow** flop is one that contains cards of all different suits. Since there are three cards in a flop, there will be one card of three different suits. The significance of a rainbow flop is that a player cannot possess a flush draw. Since each player possesses two cards, the most he can have of any one suit is three (the two in his hand and one on board). That player would need both of the remaining two cards to match his suit in order to make a flush, which is not a wise bet.

In an ideal world, you would go all-in and each of your opponents would call and you would win a huge pot.

Of course, there are very few hands that an opponent could possess that would justify him calling an all-in bet. In order to make money, you want to bet an amount that your opponent will call. You do not want her to fold. For instance, if your opponent has a hand like As6s, she would probably be willing to play for a reasonable price. She may even bet the hand herself.

Now, if the turn card brings an Ace or another spade, she will probably be willing to commit a lot more chips to the pot. By keeping her in with a reasonable bet on the flop, you give yourself the chance to make a lot more money on the turn or river. On the other hand, if you had chased her out with too large of a bet on the flop, yes, you would have won the pot but you would not have won nearly the money you should have. Remember, poker is about making money, not winning pots.

Fold Strong but Losing Hands

One of the fundamental truths of poker is that you will lose more money with strong hands than weak ones. This is an easy concept to understand, but it is still hard to avoid this pitfall. A trademark of a good player is his ability to lay down strong but losing hands.

It's often said the worst hand in poker is the second best one, because that's the hand that will be hard to lay down and it won't win. Inexperienced players often fail to see the danger and heed the warning signs of when they are in trouble.

Every hand you play has to be viewed in the context of the overall game and what your opponents may likely be holding. There will be plenty of times when the measly one pair you hold will be the best, and there will be plenty of other times when your flush will lose to a full house.

The worth of your hand should always be measured in terms of its relative strength to the potential holdings of your opponent. Never lose sight of that. Time and again, you'll witness players at the table say they know they're beat but they have to call anyway because their hand is just too good to lay down.

That's not smart poker. Poker is such a great game because it is played against others. Recognizing when you are beat will save you a lot of money. If you can never lay down strong but losing hands, you will never be a winning player.

Make Your Opponents Pay

One of the paradoxes of poker is that it is often more risky to bet a little than to bet a lot. Intuitively, the preceding sentence does not make a lot of sense to the beginning player. The novice would rather check or weakly bet a hand that is vulnerable. If a hand is vulnerable, however, that's exactly why you should make a big bet. Let's look at an example to illustrate.

Say you call a player in middle position that raises and you call from the big blind with Jd10d. You see a flop heads-up with the initial raiser. The flop comes Js6c5s. You most likely have the best hand right now with top pair. This board presents some potential problems, however. Your opponent could be holding two spades, in which case he already has four to a flush. Or he could have a hand like 7-8 in which case he has an open-ended straight draw. Even if he has a hand like A-Q, if an Ace or Queen comes on the turn or river, he'll beat you. So, you reason, with two cards still to come you better not risk a lot here.

The fact that there are two cards to come is even more reason why you should make a significant bet here. You want to make it expensive for your opponent to try and outdraw you. You don't want to make it easy for him. By giving him a free card, you are greatly increasing the chances that you will lose the hand.

You've heard the expression "the price of poker just went up." That's what you want to do here. A fundamental principle of poker is to put pressure on your opponents and force them into difficult decisions. By making a significant bet, you force your opponent to decide if it's worth calling to try and improve to the best hand. You want to bet enough so that it's not worth it. In a situation like this where it is hard to pinpoint your opponent's exact hand, it's best to bet an amount equal to at least the size of the pot.

The Price Is Not Right

If you price him out and he still calls, so be it. You have made the correct decision and you have forced your opponent to make a mistake. In the long run, that is a profitable proposition for you even if you don't win the hand. I know that will be little consolation when the fifth spade falls on the river, but keep in mind that if you keep making correct decisions and your opponents keep making mistakes, you are eventually going to win a lot of money from them.

Shame on You

On the other hand, if you do not bet enough to price him out of his draw, then he would be correct in calling you. For instance, say you have top pair on the flop with you holding AdKd and the flop coming Kc10c4s. Your opponent has 7c8c. There are nine remaining clubs that can make him a flush. Remembering the Rule of Four (nine outs multiplied by four) gives your opponent approximately a 36 percent chance of making his flush.

If you bet $10 into a $40 pot, your opponent is justified in calling you and should call you. With $50 now in the pot and only $10 to call, your opponent is getting paid 5 to 1 on his money when his odds of winning are less than that. He is making the correct decision and whether he makes his flush or not, you have made a mistake in giving him the opportunity to do so without making him pay sufficiently for it. In the immediate example, if you had bet $40 instead of $10, it would cost your opponent $40 to call a pot now equal to $80 (the original $40 plus your $40 bet). He is now only getting 2 to 1 on his money when his odds of winning are greater than that.

Hold 'em

Opponents are more likely to give a lot of weight to your last action. If you have been playing tight all night but you just got caught bluffing, it's probably wise to tighten up again. That bluff will stick in your opponents' minds more than your previous tight play.

Sizing Up the Game

We previously learned the importance of reading individual opponents. If you're paying attention and can ascertain the general style of your opponent, you can make adjustments to exploit him. It's equally important to have a reading on the overall table. If you're going to make money in poker, you have to put yourself in a position to do so, and one of the best ways to accomplish that is to adjust to the play of the table in order to maximize your expected profit.

Every poker table will have its own unique texture. Some games will be tight, some loose, some well played, and some sloppily played. If you take two $1–$2 no-limit Hold 'em tables right next to each other, one table may average pots over $50 every hand while the next one may average under $30. Some of that may be attributable to extenuating circumstances (such as a lot of contested pots featuring two or more strong hands), but usually it will be symptomatic of the players involved.

Knowing what type of game you are in will allow you to make the appropriate adjustments. Many poker pundits will advise that you should play tighter than usual in a loose game and looser than usual in a tight game. That's not quite right, but let's take a closer look.

Fold 'em

It's a lot tougher to bluff two or more players than it is to bluff just one. The more players in the pot, the more likely it is you will run into someone with a reason to call.

A Little Bit Looser Now

In a loose game, it's wise to play a little bit looser than you normally would—but not much. A loose game is one in which four or more players are routinely seeing flops. These games are action games and the pots will tend to be big with so many players involved. With so many players seeing a flop, the odds increase greatly that one or more players will hit at least a pair or a drawing hand.

In these games, players tend to stay with their mediocre hands longer because the game is loose and they know that their opponents could also be playing mediocre hands. The reason some pundits advocate playing tighter in these games is that when you have a strong hand, you are likely to get paid off by your loose opponents regardless of your tight image.

While that strategy may make you some money, it won't maximize your profits. With a loose table, you can afford to get involved in some more hands than usual. You won't need as strong a hand as you would in a tight game to make money, so the extra risk is worth it. Be careful though. Loose players are extremely contagious. There's a fine line between playing a little looser with discipline and playing reckless.

The Gutshot Straight

Good players will not only recognize the texture of the play at their tables, they will choose to play at those tables where they believe they can do better. If there's not a waiting list, scout out the ideal table for your game. Even if there's not a seat available at that table, ask the floor person to call you over when a seat does become available.

Even More Loose

In a tight game, the preferable strategy is to play looser than usual. Players in these games will be reluctant to play anything less than strong hands. When their hands don't improve, they'll be willing to lay them down.

There will be a lot of pots for the taking in these games that an aggressive player can take. The astute player who has loosened up will win more than his fair share. The added bonus is that these same players are more likely to get paid when they have strong hands than their counterparts in the game. In a tight game, those playing the tightest will have a very tough time getting anyone to play with them when they do make a hand.

Hold 'em

> Some people ask me whether you should ever show your cards to your opponents like they sometimes do on TV. There are some experienced players who will do it on occasion in order to set up an opponent for later, but it is doubtful that will work—the better advice, for less experienced players, is to never show unless you have to.

Nothing Lasts Forever

The texture of the game can change over time or it can change suddenly. Opponents may make adjustments. Some games may start out tight and then loosen up as the players get bored or fall into old habits. Others may tighten up if they are losing too much money. Still, some opponents may adjust to you. One player can go on tilt and change the texture of the entire table.

Players will come and go, and with every subtraction and/or addition, things can change. Don't get complacent at the table or rely on your initial assumptions. Stay focused and make adjustments as necessary.

The Least You Need to Know

- Play some marginal hands in order to maximize your profits on your strong hands.
- Measure the strength of your hands in relation to the potential holdings of your opponents.
- Make your opponents pay to chase their draws.
- Adjust your play according to the overall play of the table.

Chapter 6

Playing Defense

In This Chapter

- A good player can be bluffed
- Beware the trap
- Fighting boredom
- Find out where you are
- Take a stand

Knowing how much to bet and when to try bluffs and finding edges to exploit are how you maximize your profits and make money at the poker table. In previous chapters, we learned specific strategies to help you take the lead and outplay your opponents. Those strategies were primarily offensive in nature.

Keep in mind that your more skilled opponents will be looking to do all of the same types of things that you will be attempting. That's why it's just as important to be a good defensive player as well. The chips you save are just as important as the chips you win. In this chapter, we will concentrate on defensive strategies.

It Doesn't Pay to Be Cynical

If you recall back in Chapter 2, we discussed how you shouldn't try to bluff a sucker. Suckers are overly cynical and will call any bet. A corollary to that generalization is that good players can be bluffed.

If a good player can be bluffed, then there is certainly no shame in being bluffed. Beginning players have a tendency to believe that bluffing is more prevalent than it really is. They also think that the biggest sin in poker is to fall victim to a bluff. While no one likes to be bluffed out of a pot, it will cost you a lot of money to call every time you think an opponent might be bluffing.

Save Your Chips

If you do not have a decent hand, then it's pointless to even consider calling a bluff. Even if your opponent is bluffing, she could still have you beat. Your only choices in that situation are to raise or fold. By raising, you put the pressure on your opponent.

In poker, you do not want to be the one facing tough decisions. You want to force your opponents to face tough decisions. So if your hand is not strong enough to raise with, it's probably not strong enough to call with. Save those chips for a situation where you can be the one betting or raising and putting the pressure on your opponents.

Say you raise pre-flop with a pair of 7s from late position. The big blind calls and the flop comes 10-8-2. The big blind checks and you make a bet. The big blind then check raises you. You suspect that the big blind thinks you were trying to steal the pot and that he doesn't have anything. This is purely a hunch on your part.

It's simply not worth calling. Your opponent could very easily have you beat and even if he has a hand like J-9 or Q-J, he could still outdraw you. Plus, you must think ahead. If you do call, there is a great chance that your opponent will bet again no matter what the turn card brings. Unless that turn card is a 7, you will face another big decision. And, if you do call the turn, you can safely assume you will face another big bet on the river.

Always think ahead when you make a call. If it's not on the river, you will be facing more bets down the road. Rather than call that raise or the flop, save your money for a situation where you can be the aggressor and put your opponent to the test and let him face big decisions.

You Don't Have to Play Policeman

You will often hear inexperienced players call bets when they are beaten and say something like "Well, I had to keep him honest." Poker is a game of deception. Get used to it. Implement it when you can. If you have been studying your opponents and know when they are bluffing, then use that to your advantage.

However, you do not need to do the table's dirty work. If an aggressive player makes a bet and two players fold in front of you, you may feel pressure to call in order to keep the aggressive player honest. That's not your job. Of course, the rest of the table wants you to call so they can see what the aggressive player has and perhaps slow him down for future hands.

It's not their chips, though. Those chips are yours and you should only be willing to spend them when it is to your advantage to do so. Don't give in to peer pressure. Those players urging you to call weren't willing to do it with their own money.

 The Gutshot Straight

Chris Ferguson, a top professional poker player, makes a habit of taking a set amount of time to act every time the action gets to him. This affords him the opportunity to think through the situation without giving away any tells.

Take Your Time

Poker is a game of reaction. You must react to your cards, the moves of your opponents, and what's showing on the board. In addition, you must anticipate what will result from any move you make.

Poker has often been likened to a chess match, and if you have ever watched chess you know that players will take their time before they make a move.

Of course, in chess, players are not worried about giving away tells.

While not wanting to give off a *tell* is an admirable goal, it's not worth rushing into a move. The most important thing you can do at the poker table is to make the correct decision. Coming to that correct decision will often require some thought on your part. Nothing should jeopardize that thought process.

Definition

A **tell** is a nuance or mannerism a player may display that offers insight into his hand. For instance, many amateurs will stare down an opponent when they are bluffing.

If an opponent moves all-in on you, unless you have the nuts, you should take your time. Replay the hand in your mind to determine what your opponent is most likely holding. Taking your time will accomplish the following:

- It puts pressure on your opponent and whether you call or fold, he'll think twice about making such a move on you next time.

- Your opponent may give off a tell due to the pressure that he is under.

- It makes no difference if you give off a tell since your opponent has already committed all of his chips.

Look Ahead

Whenever it is your turn to act, think ahead. What will you do on the next card? Be prepared so that you are ready to act. For instance, say you raise pre-flop with AsQd and the big blind calls. The flop comes Js7s2h and your opponent bets out. You decide to call since you have two over cards. In addition, you believe that if any spade comes, you will also bet or raise and try to represent to your opponent that you have made a spade flush.

By thinking ahead, you are setting up a consistent story to your opponent. While you are hoping for an Ace or a Queen to come, you are willing to bet if any spade comes as well. You are playing the hand consistent with a flush draw. Since you have the Ace of spades, you know your opponent cannot possess the best possible flush hand.

 Hold 'em

> You should never make your mind up as to what you are going to do until it is your turn to act. Since poker is a game of imperfect information, you want to glean every possible bit of information available in order to make a correct decision. A good way to ensure you do this pre-flop is to not even look at your cards until the action gets to you. Your cards are not going to change anyway, and you can use that time to study your opponents as they look at their cards.

Hooked Like a Fish

As we learned before, deception can take many forms and bluffing is only one of them. Opponents who are adept at setting traps can cost you a lot more money than the player who bluffs.

The name of the game in poker is making money, not winning pots. Just as you will be trying to get as many chips as you can with your strong hands, so will your opponents. They will try to hide the strength of their hands hoping to induce you to try and win the pot. If you are playing aggressive poker and trying to win uncontested pots, this could present a problem. How do you balance your desire to win pots against avoiding falling victim to a trap?

While every player is unique, there are some general tactics players will use to set traps. The most obvious is that players will check or just call when they would normally bet or raise. Say a player raises in early position and two players call him. The flop comes J-6-3 and the raiser now checks. Most players will automatically bet this flop no matter what if they had raised pre-flop.

By just checking, warning signs should go off. If you do bet and that opponent just calls, then that should be another warning sign that should confirm that this player has a real strong hand such as pocket Jacks that have given him three Jacks. Players slow play these hands in the hopes that an opponent will bet into them. Even if an opponent checks, they hope that subsequent cards will give their opponents a hand worth betting.

More experienced players are willing to slow play hands throughout if they feel they can trap an opponent. The most famous example of this occurred at the very end of the main event of the 1987 World Series of Poker. Johnny Chan flopped a straight and checked it all the way through the river even though he risked not winning much money by doing so. Having set the trap, though, Erik Seidel took the bait and moved all-in on the river. It was the key hand for Johnny Chan on his way to victory.

Play Small Ball

One way to avoid getting hit too badly by a trap is to keep the pot small. If something smells fishy, make a smaller bet than you normally would. Not only will this save you money instantly, it will help you down the line.

Say your opponent raises from late position and you call in the big blind with Js10s. The flop comes Jc8c2h. You make a pot-size bet and your opponent calls. This opponent is normally aggressive and his call sets off a warning signal. The turn brings the 3s. Rather than make another pot-size bet, think about making a bet half that big. This will make it easier for you to get away from the hand if your opponent raises you.

Keep the Focus

Poker can be a very streaky game. There will be times when you can go long stretches without getting any playable hand. You will see a steady dose of hands like 7-4, 9-3, and 8-2. During these times, it can be extremely difficult to retain your focus and discipline. It's easy to get distracted when you haven't played a hand in over an hour.

Temptation Is an Expensive Sin

When you have seen a steady diet of lousy hands, even the most marginal of hands looks playable when you receive it. If you received nothing better than 10-4 for a few rounds, the next J-9 you get will look like a monster.

Evaluate each hand independently of all others. Don't get restless. If you don't play much, you are going to want to play a lot of hands especially if you are playing primarily for entertainment. Before you give into temptation, ask yourself if it's more entertaining to win money or lose money.

Think of poker as one lifelong game. Measure your success over the long term and take pride in making correct decisions. Instead of playing that J-9 hand in the face of a raise, fold it and congratulate yourself for making a correct decision and saving yourself money.

Keep Your Eyes on the Prize

If you are folding a lot of hands, it's easy to think of poker as being boring. It's anything but. There is always something to do. If you are not in a hand, study those players who are. Try to pick up betting habits and overall styles.

In order to simplify things, pick one player in each hand to observe. Try to guess what cards he is holding based on the action. If you do this consistently instead of watching the ball game on the television across the room, you will be surprised how quickly you will start to guess correctly. By taking the time to observe, you are keeping your head in the game and giving yourself the best possible chance to win.

Fold 'em

When in doubt, fold. You will save more money folding in marginal situations than you will win by calling.

Define Your Hand

There is rarely anything to be gained by playing passive poker. Say you have Q-7 in the big blind and two players limp in. The flop comes 9-7-2 rainbow. There's a good chance you may have the best hand here. If you bet it, you stand a better chance of finding out if you do. Since there wasn't much pre-flop betting, opponents are more likely to fold in the face of a bet if the flop didn't help them.

Say there's $20 in the pot and you bet $15. One player calls. Now, you may want to slow down your betting if the turn card does not help you. By calling, that player most likely has something. Now, let's say you check the flop instead of betting $15. The opponent in last position bets $15 and you decide to call. In this situation, you don't know if that opponent has something or if he bet because everyone checked to him. You have spent the same amount of money ($15) but in the first instance, you have gained more information than in the second.

Avoid the Crying Call

If you have done a good job of defining your hand, then you can avoid the *crying call*. Let's say you raise pre-flop with AsKh and one opponent behind you calls. The flop comes AdQc4d. You bet and your opponent calls. The turn brings the 10h. You bet and your opponent calls. The river is the 6d. You bet and your opponent makes a big raise. Since you have bet the hand the entire way, it's almost a certainty that you are beat. Your opponent could have K-J for a straight, any two diamonds for a flush, or a hand like A-Q or A-10 for two pair. Folding in this situation will save you a lot of money in the long run.

Definition

A **crying call** is one made on the river when a player is fairly certain he's beat but the pot is too large and the player's hand is too strong to lay down.

When Attacked, Attack Back

We have already learned in this chapter that you don't need to call every potential bluff. It's in your interest to fold when you don't have a good hand. There is a fine line, however, between making good laydowns and allowing your opponents to walk all over you.

If opponents know you will fold unless you have a strong hand, they will attack you constantly. They will continue to bet until you finally fight back. You don't have to do this every time but be cognizant of how others perceive you. If a player in late position raises every time it's your big blind, then you will have to raise him back no matter what cards you have or he will keep doing it.

The Least You Need to Know

- Don't waste a lot of chips calling every time you think an opponent may be bluffing.
- Watch out for tricky opponents trying to trap you.
- Study your opponents even if you are not in the hand.
- Make bets to define your hand and find out where you stand in relation to your opponents.

Chapter 7

Position Is Paramount

In This Chapter

- The importance of position
- Knowledge is power
- Late position, the home of deceit
- Equalizing position

Poker is a positional game. When your opponent is forced to make a decision before you, you gain valuable information. In Texas Hold 'em, your position during a hand will remain constant for that entire hand. There are a total of four betting rounds in each hand of Hold 'em played to a show-down. The importance of having favorable (or unfavorable) position during each one of those rounds cannot be underestimated. In this chapter, we will look at how you should adjust your game to account for your position.

Sizing Up Your Seat

In Hold 'em, the later your position in relation to the dealer, the better. In a 10-handed game of Hold 'em, the three players to the left of the blinds are considered to be in early position. The next three players are in middle position. The final two players ending with the player on the button are in late position. You may have noticed that we have only accounted for 8 of the 10 players. That's because the two players in the blinds are in their own category. While they will act last before the flop, they will be in early position in each subsequent betting round.

As you can imagine, there is a huge advantage in not having to act until after you have seen what everyone else (or mostly everyone else) does. When it comes to position, having the button is your best chance to play a multitude of hands.

Poker is a game of imperfect information. The more information you can gather on your opponents, the better equipped you will be to make proper decisions. Being the last to act affords you the most information.

So what is the biggest practical difference between late position and early position? In late position, you can play a lot more hands than in early position. You will have more opportunities to bluff and to steal pots. When you are in early position, there are too many players to act behind you. Unless you have a very strong hand, it is risky to enter because someone can raise behind you.

In late position, you can play many more hands, especially if no one has raised in front of you. With few players left to act, the risk is much less that you will be raised.

Let's take a look at what hands players generally play from each position. Keep in mind that these are general guidelines and there are no absolutes in poker. First, though, it is important to learn the basic rules. Once you know the rules, it will make it much easier to know when to tweak them, bend them, and even break them as you make adjustments along the way.

Furthermore, gaining an understanding of what your opponents are likely to be playing will help you recognize bluffing and betting opportunities.

Fold 'em_____

> When in early position avoid entering a pot with any hand that you would not want to raise with, since there is a good chance there could be a raise behind you with so many players left to act.

Proceed with Caution

When you are in early position, you do not want to play anything but the very strongest hands. With so many people yet to act behind you, it is simply too risky to play lesser hands. Since you should not play any hand that cannot withstand a raise, you should go ahead and raise yourself. You do this for a couple of reasons. First, you force players behind you to fold hands that they may otherwise play. You want to keep your opponents from taking advantage of their late position. Since you are going to be first to act in every betting round, you want to narrow the field so there are not as many players behind you.

Next, if a player calls you or even raises you after you have raised from early position, you will be more likely to know what kind of hand they have. Since they will need a stronger hand to call your raise, this will help you tremendously after the flop.

So what hands should you play from early position? A-A, K-K, Q-Q, A-K suited, A-K, A-Q suited, K-Q suited, and possibly A-Q, J-J, and 10-10. As you gain experience, you can start to play some other hands such as smaller pairs (i.e, 8-8) and smaller suited connectors (i.e, J-10). The advantage of selectively playing some of these lesser hands is that your opponents are likely to put you on a bigger hand since you raised from early position. Just make sure you don't get in trouble with these hands and be prepared to fold them if you don't improve on the flop and your bets don't chase anyone out.

Loosening Up from the Middle

Playing from middle position allows you to loosen up a little bit with one big qualification. It depends on what has transpired before you. If someone has already raised in front of you, then you want to stick to the same hand requirements as you would from early position and you probably do not want to play A-Q.

Hold 'em

If you're having trouble initiating a bluff, here's something to boost your confidence. Next time you play, keep track of how many hands you win without a showdown when you are taking the lead by betting or raising. We're willing to bet that the number will be high. Since you won without a showdown, it didn't matter whether you held good cards or not. Those cards just gave you the confidence to bet or raise. The bet or raise won the hand for you.

If no one has raised in front of you, then you can play all of the hands you would in early position plus the following: J-J, 10-10, 9-9, 8-8, A-J suited, A-10 suited, Q-J suited, A-J, and J-10 suited. Again, as you gain more experience, you can play smaller pocket pairs and smaller suited connectors.

Playing with Strength

Late position is where you want to be. Taking advantage of position is critical to success in Texas Hold 'em. You can play so many hands now because you have the comfort in knowing you will be in late position for each betting round. Unless there has been a really big raise, or a number of raises, by the time the action gets to you, you can play all of the hands mentioned in both early and middle positions.

In addition, you can now play a lot more hands. Any pair or suited connector (such as 7-6s) becomes playable. You can take a lot more chances in late position but you still must have discipline. Do not play anything but the best hands if there has been a big raise or a few raises to you.

If no one has entered the pot by the time the action gets to you, then you can raise with just about anything. This is especially important if the blinds are significant and worth stealing (such as in the late stages of a tournament). You want to raise with the sole intention of forcing the blinds to fold so you can win the pot without a fight.

Even if you don't win the hand before the flop, you are in great position for the next three rounds. Your opponent will have to act first in each of those rounds and you can see his action before making your decision.

Hold 'em

The cutoff position is one to the right of the button. It is so called because a good player in this position can effectively raise to force the player on the button to fold, thereby cutting him off from the best position at the table and securing it for herself.

The Blinds: To Defend or Not

Even though the blinds act last or pre-flop, they will act first in every subsequent betting round. The bottom line is that you should play the blinds the same way you would play early position with a few exceptions.

First, if you are in the small blind, more hands are playable if no one has raised before you. Since it will only cost you another half bet, play those hands you would play in middle position and even some you would play in late position.

Next, if you are in the big blind, then you get a free look at the flop if no one has raised before you. If there is a raise, then treat the hand the same way you would early position.

You will hear a lot about defending the blinds. What does that mean? Well, we just saw that one of the benefits of late position is the ability to steal the blinds. If the blinds are worth stealing, then it would seem to make sense that they are worth defending. This is only partly true. The fact is that you will still be out of position in each subsequent betting round. Additionally, your opponent in late position will not always be on a steal. The bottom line is that you will occasionally have to defend your blinds in order to send a message to the rest of the table that they cannot just steal at will. Do not get carried away with this practice, though, as it can get expensive. You are better off saving those chips for an opportunity to steal the blinds yourself when you are in late position.

If you're going to defend a position, then defend the button. When you are on the button, be prepared to call some raises, especially from players in late position who may be trying to force you to fold so they have the best position. Look at the blinds as your cost of doing business. Once those chips are posted, they're no longer yours. Doesn't it make more sense to defend late position than early position?

Information Is Critical

Poker is a game of imperfect information. While you will know your cards and the common cards, you will not know your opponents' cards. You can, however, gain insight to the potential hands your opponent holds based on their actions from a certain position.

Look to Your Right

When you sit down to the poker table, take a good look at the three players to your immediate right. While you should be paying attention to the entire table, focus on these players specifically. Watch their eyes instead of the cards when the dealer turns over the flop. Study what hands they are willing to play from which position. Will they continue to bet a hand even if they miss the flop? What will they do in the face of a raise?

Why all of the attention to these three players? Because these are the players you have favorable position over. These are the players who will consistently act before it is your turn to act. You will have the upper hand when it comes to gaining information. Most important, you will have the best chance to win money from these opponents more than the other players at the table.

Beware of Your Left

Once you have finished your review of the three players to your right, study the three players to your left. These are the players that will have favorable position on you. You will consistently be at a disadvantage when you enter pots against them. Since these are the players you are most likely to lose money to, answer the following questions about each of them:

- How aggressive are they?
- How important is position to them?
- Do they always defend their blinds?
- Will they consistently raise when they are in late position?
- Do they bully players in front of them?

The more aggressive they are, the more careful you will have to be. You don't want to enter with hands you are not willing to call a raise with. If the players to your left are overly aggressive, try trapping them. Limp in with your strong hands such as A-A, K-K, A-K, and Q-Q, and then wait for them to raise. Once they do, make a big re-raise.

Pick Your Seat Wisely

In most poker games, you will be given a seat as one opens up in the game of your choice. Sometimes, however, there will be more than one seat open at a table. Other times, after you have been playing for a while, another seat at the table may open up.

If you have a choice, pick a seat where the weaker players will be to your right. These are the players you want to exploit and make money from. Having position on them will give you the best chance to accomplish that.

Hold 'em

If you're winning most of your hands without a showdown, you're probably playing too conservatively. Loosen up and take advantage of your tight image to steal some pots.

Bluffing from Late Position

From late position, the game really opens up. You can play a lot more hands increasing your chances of hitting a flop and making a strong hand. Since the hands you can play from late position vary greatly, the strength of your hand will often be well hidden. For instance, say you are able to limp in from late position with the 3h4h. The flop comes 9-3-3. A player in middle position with a hand like a pair of tens or A-9 will feel confident that he has the best hand, and you stand to win a lot of money.

The beauty of playing from late position is that it will be very difficult for your opponents to define your hand. Because you are forced to only play strong hands from early position, it is easier for opponents to narrow the range of hands you could be playing when you enter the pot from early position. In late position, opponents will know that you could be playing a wide variety of hands which opens up a lot of opportunities for you.

For example, say you are in late position with 8d9d in a $5–$10 game. A tight, aggressive opponent open raises under the gun for $30. You call since you have position. The flop comes 3d5h7h. Your opponent bets the flop. There is a great likelihood that this flop did not help your opponent at all. However, your opponent knows that you probably know that. So, if you raise, he may think you are trying to steal. Instead of raising here, just call the bet.

If you did have a strong hand, you would probably just call here so your opponent is likely to believe you. Now, say the turn brings the 4d. Even though that card did not help you, your opponent may believe it did. There are now four cards to a straight. Any player holding a 6 would have a straight. There is a much greater chance that you would have a 6 playing from late position than he would playing from early position. In this scenario, it is highly likely that your opponent will check the turn and fold when you bet.

Those kinds of situations occur all the time and the player in late position is the one who can best take advantage. Here is a good tidbit to keep in mind. For any player who starts with an unpaired hand, the odds of making at least one pair or better on the flop are less than 33 percent. That means if you are in late position against only one other opponent, there is a very good chance for you to make a move.

Let's look at another possible scenario. Say two players limp in right in front of you. You make a standard pre-flop raise from the button with Ac4c. The conditions are right for a bluff—i.e., you haven't been bluffing often; the players are relatively tight; there's no one with a huge stack, a very small stack, or on tilt; and your table image is conservative. The 8sQh2d flop completely misses you, but it's checked to you, indicating (unless someone's slow playing) that no one has a Queen. This is a good spot for a bet of half to three quarters of the pot. Some would call that a continuation bet, but it's at least equally valid to call it a bluff because there's a good chance that you don't have the best hand.

Hold 'em

Cultivating the right table image at the poker table can make life a lot easier and win you a lot of pots. When opponents respect your play and are intimidated by you, they will try to avoid confrontations with you.

Again, here's where position works for you and against your opponents. They probably called your pre-flop raise with high cards, pocket pairs, or suited connectors. It's very unlikely that anyone flopped two pairs. Apparently no one has a Q, and how can someone with 9-8, 8-7, J-10, 10-9, A-2 suited call out of position? Of course, if someone raises, you fold. If someone calls, they may be slow playing and it might be a good idea to put on the brakes.

Making the Best of Early Position

Early position is a tough place to play from. It is not hopeless, however. Astute players learn tricks to make the most of their early position depending on the situation and their opponents. If you have been studying your opponents to the left of you, you can try a few things.

Checking Doesn't Mean Surrendering

As we learned in the previous example, many players will check the flop from early position if their hand hasn't improved. This is a conservative strategy that will keep you from squandering chips. You can't, however, always allow your late position opponents to take the pot every time you miss a flop. Remember that there is a good chance that they may have missed the flop as well. In addition, you may have the better hand since you probably needed a better hand to play with from an earlier position.

If you find that every time you check, an opponent will bet, you have to take matters into your own hands. Try a check-raise as both an offensive and defensive strategy. For example, say you raise from middle position with Ad10d. One player behind you calls. The flop comes Js8d4c. You check and your opponent bets. Rather than fold, raise. Since a check-raise would have been a way to extract value out of a hand like A-J, your opponent is likely to believe you have a strong hand. That serves your offensive purpose. You also send a strong message to the entire table that you will check-raise from early position. They will realize that when you check in the future, they are not free to steal the pot. This will allow you to see some turn and river cards for free and even check down a hand like Ad10d that may ultimately be the winning hand.

The Great Equalizer

As we've learned, position is critical because you will either act before or after your opponent on every betting round. What if there were no further betting rounds? Then late position would no longer have an advantage. Of course, we can't change the rules of poker to suit our position. There is one tool available to you, though, that can accomplish the same thing.

If you move all-in, there will be no more betting rounds for you. There are no further decisions to be made. There is no more advantage to being the last to act. Once that all-in bet is made, the players following are now at a distinct disadvantage. They face a big decision. If they call, the only way they can win is if they have the best hand or draw to the

The Gutshot Straight

When up against better competition, especially in tournaments, the all-in move can be very effective. It not only neutralizes position, it closes the talent gap. Professionals hate it when amateurs move all-in on them because it puts all of the pressure on the professionals and it takes away the professional's advantage to outplay their amateur opponents as the amateur has no other decision to make.

best hand. They can no longer use their position to bet or raise.

So when should the all-in move from early position be made? The all-in bet should be used sparingly and should be used when there is money to be made. The fundamentals of bluffing, deception, or

Definition

Value betting is a bet made for profit. The bettor wants to get called because she is confident that she has the superior hand.

value betting learned earlier should be considered. If you have been playing tight and have a conservative table image, the time is right.

Say you are in a tournament with the blinds at $400 and $800 with $100 antes. There are 10 players at the table so the pot is $2,200 before anyone acts. You have $3,000 in chips and are in early position. The players in the blinds have about $5,000 in chips. You look at your cards and see 10s9s. Not a good hand to play from early position, but you will soon have to post the blinds and your stack will take a significant hit.

This is a good situation to move all-in. Your opponents are likely to give you credit for a good hand and they will have a hard time calling with anything less than A-K, A-A, K-K, Q-Q, J-J, or 10-10.

The Least You Need to Know

- Poker is a positional game and there is a tremendous advantage in being last to act.
- Look to make money from the players to your right.
- Be careful of tricky players on your left.
- Defend your button more than your blinds because when you are on the button you are in the best position.
- Moving all-in can take away an opponent's position advantage and talent advantage.

Tournament Play

In This Chapter

- The action is forced
- Be on high alert
- Don't wait until it's too late
- Beware the large stack
- … and the short stack, too

If you're new to poker, you've probably been introduced through the magic of television. Poker has exploded in the last few years due to the great popularity of tournaments. Tournaments differ greatly from traditional cash games.

In a cash game, some players will be winners and some will be losers. Among the winners, some will be big winners and some will be small. In a tournament, play continues until one person has all of the chips. The chips used in a tournament have no value outside of the tournament. Once you pay your entry fee, the only way to walk away a winner is to advance far into the tournament.

There are some subtle but very significant strategic differences in how you should approach a tournament. In this chapter, we're going to take a look at what those differences are and how you can bet and bluff your way to victory.

Hold 'em

When you enter a tournament, you will notice a fee that will be something like $100 + $15. The $100 is the amount that goes into the prize pool while the $15 represents the casino's take for hosting the event.

The Blinds Keep Going Up

If you sit down to a $1–$2 cash game, you can rest assured that the blinds will stay the same all night. In a tournament, the blinds will increase at regular predetermined intervals. Let's take a look at a sample tournament structure:

Level	Ante	Blinds	Duration
1		$25–$50	20 minutes
2		$50–$100	20 minutes
3		$100–$200	20 minutes
4	$25	$150–$300	20 minutes
5	$50	$200–$400	20 minutes
6	$75	$300–$600	20 minutes
BREAK			20 minutes

Level	Ante	Blinds	Duration
7	$100	$500–$1,000	20 minutes
8	$100	$800–$1,600	20 minutes
9	$200	$1,000–$2,000	20 minutes
10	$300	$2,000–$4,000	20 minutes
11	$500	$3,000–$6,000	20 minutes
12	$1,000	$5,000–$10,000	20 minutes

This would be a typical structure for a daily tournament where each player starts with around $3,000 in chips. In the first level, you would have plenty of chips to play with, as it will only cost you $75 a round (you would pay each of the blinds once per round).

However, in the fourth round, which would occur after only 60 minutes of play, it would cost you $700 a round. You would pay each of the blinds once per round and the ante every hand, so assuming 10 players per table that would be $150 + $300 + (10 × $25). This is a big difference. Assuming that you maintained your $3,000 in starting chips for the first hour, you would find yourself with a rapidly decreasing stack.

In a cash game, you can afford to wait for good opportunities. Good players will often observe and play very few hands the first hour in order to get a feel for their opponents and the texture of the game. In a tournament, you don't have the luxury of waiting too long.

The Gutshot Straight

In the 2006 main event of the World Series of Poker, well over 8,000 players paid $10,000 each to enter, resulting in a first-place prize of $12,000,000.

Go for the Money

In a poker tournament, every player pays the same entry fee and begins with the same amount of chips. Once you are out of chips, you are eliminated from the tournament. Play continues until everyone is eliminated but one player. That player ends up with all of the chips. The chips in play do not represent actual dollar amounts but only serve as a way of keeping score in the tournament. So the winner of the tournament typically does not win all of the money even though he ends up with all of the chips. (If there are only a handful of players in the tournament, then the winner may take all of the money.)

As a general rule, players finishing in the top 10 percentile will be "in the money." For example, if 100 people enter a tournament, the final 10 players will each win money. The amount each receives will be weighted heavily toward how high they finish. The tenth-place finisher will get not much more than her entry fee back, while the first-place finisher may end up with as much as a third of the entire pool of money.

Let's look at a sample payout structure for a tournament where there are 300 players and each player paid an entry fee of $100 (plus $15 for the casino). There is a total prize pool of $30,000 and the top 27 finishers will get paid. A typical payout structure would be as follows:

Place	Finished	Winnings as a % of Prize Pool
1	$10,410	34.7%
2	$4,800	16.0%
3	$2,550	8.5%
4	$1,800	6.0%
5	$1,350	4.5%
6	$1,050	3.5%
7	$750	2.5%
8	$600	2.0%
9	$480	1.6%
10–18	$390 each	1.3%
19–27	$300 each	1.0%

From studying this payout structure, you can see that only a handful of people out of 300 entrants will make the really significant money. It's important to keep this in mind as we discuss tournament strategy. The goal should not be to survive as long as possible. The goal should be to finish in the top few places.

Play to Win

Anyone can sit down to a tournament and play ultra conservatively and outlast at least half of the field. Beginning players often confuse what constitutes success in a tournament. In a 300-person tournament, the player who finishes in 100th place fared no better than the player who finished in 286th. In fact, our 100th-place finisher may have actually played worse if he never gave himself a chance to win.

In a cash game, you can be a winning player by playing solid conservative poker without bluffing much or taking unnecessary risks. In a tournament, that will not be the case. Because of the increasing blinds, the action is forced. Players who are unable to increase their stack will be eliminated. Unless you happen to get a lot of good hands, you're going to have to make some things happen in order to win.

The bluffing, deception, and betting strategies that you learned in previous chapters will still work here, but there are a number of fundamental differences of which you should be aware. First, you will have to bluff more. Second, your opponents are likely to bluff more as well since they will be in the same position. Finally, your opponents will be more alert to your potential bluffs.

The fact that your opponents may put you on a bluff doesn't mean that they will call. The fact that once a player is out of chips, he is eliminated from the tournament serves as a big deterrent to players

calling bluffs even if they suspect one. In the rest
of this chapter, we'll look at the primary factors
to consider when it comes to making big bets or
implementing a bluff. Even if you are primarily a
cash game player, you should play the occasional
tournament, as it will help develop your betting and
bluffing tactics.

The Gutshot Straight

A freeroll is poker slang for a tournament
that does not cost you a dime to enter.

Keeping Up with the Game

We already discussed the importance of staying
focused on the opposition during a poker game.
The number of factors to keep abreast of in a tournament increases exponentially.

Let's start with the other players at your table. In
a cash game, you may play all night with the same
players or at least the majority of them. That will
give you the opportunity to study them and plan
accordingly. In a tournament, as players are eliminated, tables are consolidated. The tournament
director will be in charge of moving players.

As you advance throughout a tournament, you are
likely to find yourself continuously playing against
new players. What this means is that you will have
to size up your opponents quickly and go with your
instinct. The most important factor to pay attention
to is the size of your chip stack.

Working with Few Chips

If you have ever played Texas Hold 'em, you will know that there are plenty of times that you find very few or even no hands to play in an hour's time. If we get off to such an unfortunate start in a tournament, we could find ourselves in a lot of trouble rather quickly. Using our hypothetical structure, our $3,000 starting stack is a comfortable amount at Level 1. At Level 4, we would be entering the danger zone if we still had $3,000. By Level 7, that same $3,000 stack would inspire desperation. See if you can figure out how much each round would cost us in blinds and antes in Level 7. The answer is at the end of the next paragraph.

You may ask, "Wouldn't everybody else be in the same position?" The answer is no. Poker tournaments are Darwinian in nature. Only the fit survive. And in tournament poker, the large stacks are the fittest. By Level 4, quite a few players will have been eliminated. Let's assume that in our tournament, 50 percent of the players are gone by then. The average chip stack would then be $6,000. We started with 300 players with $3,000 in chips each. That's a total of $900,000 in chips.

With 150 players left, the average stack would be $6,000 (900,000 ÷ 150). Of course, not every player will have $6,000 in chips. Some will have much more. Many will have less. Those players with less will be the ones entering panic mode. Hopefully you figured out that in Level 7, each round would cost us $2,500 (the big blind of $1,000, the small blind of $500, and 10 antes at $100 each). If we want to advance, we're going to have to accumulate some chips way before then.

Hold 'em

When there are only a few more players to be eliminated before the remaining players make the money, the play often becomes very conservative. No one wants to be eliminated on the bubble just short of the money. Experienced players will exploit that time period to be aggressive and win some chips, especially against the short-stack players who are just trying to survive into the money.

The single biggest difference between playing in a tournament as opposed to a cash game is the incremental increase in the blinds and the introduction of antes. In a cash game, you would never be forced to play with a small stack. You would either buy more chips or walk away from the table.

Tournaments are an entirely different animal. If you are going to play them, you are going to have to learn to adjust. If you do not think ahead you are doomed. That's why it is so important to study the blind structure ahead of time. You need to know how much time you have before you are in the danger zone. Once you know that, you will want to try and accumulate some chips before you get in trouble.

Before the tournament starts, ask for a copy of the blind and ante structure. While you are playing, make sure you always know how much time is left in the current level and what the blinds and antes will be in the next level.

Make Your Move

The news is not all bad, though. There is a flip side to the increasing blinds and antes. At the bigger levels, there are more chips in the pot to win. For example, if everyone folds to you on the button during Level 1 and you successfully raise to steal the blinds, you will win $75. Make that same move in Level 4 and you scoop $700. You can increase your chip stack quickly at these later levels.

In a cash game, the blinds stay static and are never worth risking your entire stack to steal. If you are playing a $1–$2 cash game, it may be worth a $5 bet to pick up the $3 in blinds, but you wouldn't risk $100. In a tournament, with the blinds and antes increasing, they become worth a steal attempt.

If you're going to try and steal them, however, you have to have enough chips to scare off your opponents. As a general rule of thumb, if your stack dips below 10 times the amount of the big blind, you should be looking for opportunities to steal. If everyone folds to you in late position, you should raise to three or four times the big blind with any two cards.

Once your stack gets close to five times the big blind, your only move is to push all-in if you are going to play a hand. Look to play any two big cards or a medium pair or higher from early position and any two cards if everyone folds to you in late position. The key is to be the first person to bet so you increase the chances of everyone else folding.

The best defense, however, is a good offense. Before you get down to 10 times the big blind, start implementing some of the deceptive practices you've learned here to increase your stack and keep yourself in good position. In poker tournaments, the bigger stacks have all the power.

Fold 'em

If you leave your seat in a tournament, your blinds and antes will still be posted in your absence—so make sure to get up only during the scheduled breaks.

Watch Out for the Bully

Like the old neighborhood bully, the big stacks in tournaments will look to take advantage of their smaller-stack brethren. Remember that the chips don't have any value outside of the tournament. Also, once you're out of chips, you can't buy any more.

The size of your opponents' chip stacks will have a great affect on the play and you must adjust accordingly. Players with big stacks are likely to play a lot of hands. They will play a lot of hands especially against the small stacks. Small stacks will be very cautious about taking on the big stacks since they know they can be eliminated very easily. In a cash game, this dynamic wouldn't exist.

Poker tournaments are a test of the survival of the fittest. Unless you have a strong hand, you want to avoid confrontations with larger stacks. They are likely to call with marginal holdings and may even raise you back. Bluffs are more prevalent in tournaments so the larger stacks may not fall for them as readily as they otherwise would.

Try your bluffs on the smaller stacks who cannot afford to squander any chips. Attack those weaker than you. Even if they suspect a bluff, they will have a hard time calling unless they have a strong hand.

When you have a big stack, don't be afraid to use it. Make sure you bully the others. It takes chips to make chips in tournament poker. When you have them, open up your starting hand requirements and bet and raise aggressively. If you do get called or raised by a smaller stack, then your opponent probably has a fairly strong hand since he is willing to take on your large stack.

Hold 'em

When players get short stacked, they are looking to double up. If they get a strong hand, they want someone with a larger stack to call with a weaker hand so they can double their chip stack.

Be Wary of the Desperate

As we have been discussing, the smaller stacks will get picked on. They are the ones who can ill afford to lose chips and risk elimination. No one wants to have their tournament lives on the line with a hand like 9-4 offsuit.

Every small stack will reach a point of desperation, however. If your stack reaches too small a level, you have no choice but to play the hand dealt you. For instance, say you are in late position. The blinds are $500 and $1,000 with $100 antes. You only have $7,000 in chips left so you are looking for opportunities to gather some more. With $2,500 in the pot before the cards are dealt, the blinds and antes are definitely worth stealing.

Everyone folds to you on the button and you want to raise no matter what. Your cards are irrelevant. You take a peek and see that you have 7-2 offsuit but you are looking to steal. However, you notice that the big blind has only $1,200 more in her stack. She is likely to call your bet no matter what. Her stack is just way too small to keep folding.

So if you raise, you are likely to get called. If you do get called, your hand is so lousy that it will be an underdog to just about any other hand. In addition, since your opponent will be all-in, you will both be required to turn over your cards before the flop. Now, everyone at the table will see that you were trying to steal the blinds and antes with your raise. That could cost you the next time you attempt the same move.

Playing against short stacks can be a double-edged sword. You can usually push them out of pots unless they have very strong hands. On the other hand, once their stack is greatly diminished, they will be forced to play just about any hand. Finally, keep in mind that a player on the verge of being short stacked may try a move just like you would.

Pay Attention to the Clues

We started out this chapter by recognizing that it will be hard for you to get a feel for your opponents since the action will move quickly, tables will be consolidated, and you will continuously face new players.

However, by paying attention to the size of each player's stack and the levels of the blinds (both current and upcoming), you can both make adjustments to your own play and anticipate potential moves of your opponents.

The Least You Need to Know

- In tournaments, players will be bluffing more than usual since they have to keep pace with the increasing blinds.

- Stay focused on the opposition and the size of your chips.

- Try some bluffs to win some chips before your stack becomes too small.

- The biggest stacks in tournaments wield the most power and can punish the smaller stacks.

- Anticipate potential moves of your opponents by paying attention to the stack size and the levels of the blinds.

The Power of Chips

In This Chapter

- The tools of the trade
- Picking the right game
- Controlling the size of the pot
- Isolating opponents

There are a lot of surface-level contradictions in poker. Poker is a finesse game, but it is also a power game. While a player must possess discipline and self-control to be successful, he must also be willing to flex his muscle and use his chips when he has to. Poker is a game of skill but it cannot be played without some level of risk. In this chapter, we'll look at how you can develop the right attitude and use your chips to maximum advantage.

A Means to an End

When you're playing poker, you must consider your chips as a means to an end. They are your instruments for plying your trade. Treat them as an architect would his slide rule. Cherish them, savor them, but don't be afraid to use them. You can't win in poker without putting those chips at risk. If you view them solely as money, you cannot win. Instead of thinking how those chips can best be used to win a pot, you'll be thinking what those chips can buy outside of the table.

If it costs you $50 to call a bet when you're getting 5–1 pot odds when you are a 3–1 underdog, it makes sense to call. If you're focused on spending that $50 on dinner that night, you're not going to call. Remember that winning poker is all about making correct decisions. Make the right decisions and the pots will come your way. Those correct decisions will often involve risking chips that could be used to pay for things away from the table.

There is a fine balance between aggressiveness and recklessness. When you are reckless, you have a total disregard for the value of your chips. When you are aggressive, you are using the value of those chips to put maximum pressure on your opponents.

Managing Your Bankroll

It takes chips to make chips. If you're going to play poker, you need to have a sufficient bankroll before you sit down to the table. Even if you are purely a recreational player, segregate your poker funds from the rest of your money. Be willing to lose whatever amount you put into your poker bankroll.

Keep careful logs of every poker session in order to measure your success. No matter what, don't dip into other funds to supplement your poker bankroll. If you are losing more than you can afford to, then take a break until you can build your bankroll back so that you are only playing with discretionary funds.

Hold 'em

It's a good idea to maintain a separate bankroll that is used solely for poker. This will prevent you from dipping into funds needed for other purposes and will also help you to easily keep track of your poker wins and losses.

Choose the Most Profitable Game

Picking the right game is just as important as playing well. First and foremost, you must choose a game that is well within your means. If you are playing at a monetary level that makes you uncomfortable, you will have a hard time making optimal decisions. The same denomination games could vary in play greatly. For instance, there may be two tables of $1–$2 no-limit Texas Hold 'em side by side and one of the tables averages pots of $150 while the other rarely has a pot over $50.

The next factor to consider is both the skill level and types of opponents. While the lower the tables stakes, the lesser the competition is a good rule of thumb, it's not an absolute. There can be some very good players at low stakes and some sloppy players at the highest level. Save your judgments on each of your opponents until you have had the opportunity to study them in action.

If you play at the same card room on a regular basis, you should get a good feel for the types and styles of play at the different levels of play. Each individual table may stray from the norm, so remember that you always have the option of moving to a new game. If you are changing games (i.e., from a $1–$2 game to a $2–$5 game), then you will need to get on the waiting list. If you want to switch from one $1–$2 table to another one, then you should be given first priority for the next seat at the table you wish to switch to.

Don't be shy about asking to switch tables or even switching seats at your table. It's your money and time that you are investing and you should take control as to how and where you spend it.

The Gutshot Straight

There's an old poker saying that if you can't spot the sucker at the table, you're it. That may not be accurate, but if you find that other players are anxious to play pots with you and consistently raise you, you probably don't have a positive table image. If you feel you're not getting any respect, then test your table image. Make a big pre-flop raise when you are the first to enter the pot and see if you get any callers. If you do, it may be time to take a break.

Buy In for the Right Amount

Once you choose the game that's right for you, you must make a decision on how much you should buy in for. When playing no-limit, you can bet up to your entire stack at any time. The flip side is that all of the chips you have on the table are at risk. Once you buy in, you typically are not allowed to take chips off of the table.

The advantage of buying in for a large stack is two-fold. First, you can use that stack to your advantage to bully your opponents. Second, if you have a strong hand and someone is willing to pay you off, you want to make sure you maximize your profit.

The downside to buying in for a large stack is that if you are not comfortable betting that much money, it will work against you. For instance, say you sit down to a $1–$2 no-limit game. The maximum buy-in is $500, so that's how much you buy in for. The very first hand, you pick up pocket Queens on the button. There is a raise in front of you to $10. You re-raise to make it $25 total. The original raiser calls and you see the flop heads-up. The flop comes 10-9-3 rainbow. The original raiser immediately goes all-in and he has you covered.

While you think you may have the best hand, it will cost you $475 to call. You have never played with this player before and you really don't know what to make of his bet. The prudent thing would be to fold in this situation.

Now, let's suppose that instead of buying in for $500, you bought in for only $100. It would only cost you $75 to call that bet on the flop. This is a much easier call to make.

If you're just starting out, it's highly advisable to buy in for a lower amount. Since we're trying to work on making good decisions, the lower buy-in will make your decision-making process easier. When you don't have as much at stake, you won't feel as much pressure.

The most difficult decisions to make in Texas Hold 'em come after the flop. If you start with a low buy-in, you may find yourself all-in pre-flop more frequently, which again will alleviate tough decisions down the road.

As you gain experience, you will want to buy in for progressively larger amounts. Eventually, you want to get to the point where you routinely buy in for the maximum amount so long as you are completely comfortable using all of those chips when the situation calls for it. Having a large stack will allow you to make big bets and raises against your opponents and force them to make the tough decisions.

Fold 'em

When you sit down to a no-limit Hold 'em cash game, it's a good idea to have chips at least equal to 40 times the amount of the big blind. If you have less than that, try to find a less expensive game.

Keep the Pot to Your Liking

If you have a strong hand, you want to build the pot and keep players in. If you have a drawing hand to a potential winner, you want to keep the pot small until you make the hand. If you are out of position, you don't want the pot to escalate, either. Finally, if you are up against an aggressive opponent, you don't want the pot growing too quickly, either.

The larger the pot becomes, the greater the likelihood that someone will try to win it. With more at stake, players will be willing to take some risks. Keep in mind that pots can grow a couple of ways.

A lot of bets or raises will do it. However, a number of people entering the hand can increase the pot as well. If six players are in the pot, you can be looking at a substantial pot without any big raises.

Here's a common mistake you'll often see. In a $2–$5 game, five players call, making a total of $32 in the pot (the $7 in blinds plus the $25 in calls). The next player to act raises $5 with his pocket 8s. That's a big mistake. A $5 raise is not going to chase anyone out now that the pot has escalated. And now when the action goes back around, there is a good chance that someone will make a large raise to try and now win the substantial pot. So, instead of seeing a flop in a large pot for $5, that player will now be forced to fold after investing $10. Always think in terms of the size of the pot when you make a raise.

Make It Head's Up

Some hands play better against one or two opponents than a number of opponents. Drawing hands such as 7s8s are hands you want to enter with multiple players in the pot. That is because these hands have the potential to make strong hands such as straights or flushes, and they can bring you a lot of money if and when you make that hand.

Starting hands like big to medium pocket pairs are best played with only one or two other opponents. That is because while you likely have the best hand before the flop, your hand is unlikely to improve.

If you allow a lot of opponents in the pot, then you are greatly increasing the chances that your hand will not hold up.

So if you start with big pocket pairs, the goal should be to bet enough to isolate one opponent or win the pot right there before the flop. Never be disappointed with a win no matter how small. Even if you have pocket Aces, be glad to win a small pot. It's better to win a small pot than lose a large one.

Hold 'em

A family pot is one where most, if not all, of the players at the table have entered.

Raise It Up

If you have pocket Aces, Kings, or Queens, you should always raise when you enter a pot. With Aces, you obviously already have the best hand. You will be a big favorite against any other hand, but you will be an underdog against three or more hands collectively. What's worse is that you will have a hard time folding your hand if you are beat.

For instance, say you limp in with Aces from middle position hoping to trap, hiding the strength of your hand. You get three callers behind you. Since none of your opponents raised, it's fairly certain that none of them has a big pocket pair. The flop comes 9s8c3s. If someone bets into you or raises your bet, the hands they could be holding are varied. They could have a flush or a straight draw. Or they could have a hand like A-9—which you have dominated—or a hand like 9-9, 8-8, or 9-8, in which case you are in a lot of trouble.

By not raising pre-flop with your pocket Aces, you invite trouble. Not only do you allow drawing hands to stick around, you are going to have a hard time figuring out what your opponent has. Remember, hands like 8-7 suited play best in multi-way pots when you can see a flop cheaply. If you make a big raise before the flop, you are only going to get one or two callers and it won't be worth it for the 8-7 suited hand to play.

Say in the previous example, you raised with your Aces and only got one caller. Now, when that flop comes 9s8c3s, you can have greater confidence that your opponent missed the flop.

With Kings or Queens, there is a great likelihood that you have the best hand. You want to play them like Aces pre-flop. Again, the important thing here is not only to thin the field of opponents, but to gain knowledge. Unlike Aces, Kings or Queens are vulnerable to a higher card coming on the flop. By raising with a hand like Queens, you keep an opponent from playing a hand like A-10. This reduces the chance of an Ace on the flop beating you. If you do get called, you will still have to fear a hand like A-K. So, if an Ace or King does come on the flop, bet and see what reaction you get. If you get called or raised, you are most likely beat and it's time to give up on the hand.

With smaller pairs such as 8-8 or below, it's usually best to treat them as drawing hands. Try to see a flop cheaply. If you happen to make a set, then you can win a big pot. The exception to this is if you have one of these pairs in late position and everyone has folded to you. Now, you should play them like a bigger pair and try to force opponents out. Even if you get called by one opponent, there is a good chance you have the best hand. You can treat your hand like a big pair and continue to bet the flop no matter what. Your opponent is likely to give you credit for higher cards, so she will be looking to fold unless she hits the flop.

Hold 'em

The advantage of a large stack is even greater in tournaments because anyone with a smaller stack risks elimination going up against you.

The Intimidation Factor

A big stack can be intimidating. That's one reason why your ultimate goal should be to sit down at a table with a maximum buy-in. More important than having them is letting the players at the table know that you are not afraid to use them.

Pick a spot to show your weight even where it's not necessary. For instance, say you have $300 in front of you and you raise to $20 in late position with pocket Jacks; the big blind calls you. The flop comes 10-7-2 rainbow. The big blind bets $30, leaving him only $50 left. You have $280 left, so you can raise him $50 and put him all-in and you would still have $200 left. Rather than do that, state that you're all-in and push your entire stack in the middle of the table. Even though you are only risking $80 of that $280, the psychological effect of pushing a big stack in can be damaging to all of the other players.

The Least You Need to Know

- Keep a separate poker bankroll of funds not needed for anything else to help you play within your means and measure your success rate.

- When selecting a game, be sure to buy in for an amount that you feel comfortable with and that will maximize your profits.

- With strong starting hands, bet enough to narrow the field down to one opponent to avoid giving others the chance to outdraw you.

- Let your opponents know that you are not afraid to use your chips in order to intimidate them.

Advanced Strategies

In This Chapter

- Check raising
- Advanced bluffs
- Advanced river play
- Final adjustments

We've learned the fundamentals to bluffing and betting for optimal value; now it's time to take your game to the next level. Poker is a game of constant adjustments and thinking one step ahead of your opponents. In this chapter, we'll take a look at certain strategies to help you mix up your play, outwit your opponents, and win some money. Finally, we'll get you in the proper mind-set so you can learn to anticipate the moves of other players and keep one step ahead of them.

A Move for All Occasions

One of the most powerful tools in poker is the check raise. When you are in early position, you check the flop, turn, or river and let your opponents act first. When an opponent does bet and the action gets back to you, you raise. This move is often associated with trapping with a monster hand, but it is much more diverse than that.

The check raise can be used for bluffing, value betting, or drawing. It can also be used to effectively neutralize position. If you have some aggressive opponents to your left who like to bet a lot, the check raise is a good defensive measure to slow them down. We discussed trapping previously in Chapter 3, so let's take a look at some of the other ways it can be implemented.

 Hold 'em_____

If you call on the river only to see your opponent turn over the winning hand, take your cards and muck them, which is to toss them face down to the dealer. Don't allow your opponents to see your cards if you don't have to show them.

The Check Raise Value Play

Let's suppose you are in the big blind with Ad10c playing a $2–$5 no-limit game. A tight aggressive player in middle position open raises to $10.

Everyone folds to you and you call the extra $5 bet. The flop comes 10d6d2h. You have top pair with top kicker, so you are fairly confident that you have the best hand. While there are two diamonds on the board, you have the Ace of diamonds. Thus, even if your opponent has two diamonds, he has to fear the Ace.

Now, you know that your opponent most likely has two big cards such as A-K or K-Q. This is not a hand you want to slow play. You want to win it right here on the flop and not take any chances of your opponent outdrawing you. If you make a pot-sized bet, you'll probably win the $22 in the pot. However, if you check, you know your opponent will make a continuation bet even if he's missed the flop.

So you check and, sure enough, he bets $15. There's now $37 in the pot and you raise him another $25. He folds. Instead of winning $22, you have just won $37 by check raising. The goal was still the same. The idea here was to value bet the flop and take the pot down. By check raising, you won an extra bet.

The Check Raise Bluff

The bread and butter of the check raise is to trap an opponent with a monster hand. If you get to see a flop from the big blind with pocket 8s and the flop comes A-8-2, you can win a big pot from someone holding a hand like A-Q. They will be motivated to win the pot with their top pair, and will bet to do so.

Put yourself in the mind of your opponent. If she sees you implement a check raise, what's the first thought that will go through her mind? She'll think that you are sitting on a monster pile of hands that's trapping her.

Say a couple of players limp in and you get to see a flop for free from the big blind holding J-9. The flop comes 8-5-2 rainbow. This is the type of flop that is unlikely to have helped anybody but you. Since you are in the big blind, you could have any random hand. Of course, this flop didn't help you. The typical move in this case, though, is to bet out like it did help you.

This is where the chess match starts. Your opponents are apt to be cynical and they may believe you are trying to steal the pot by making a typical big blind move. However, if you check raise here, they are more likely to believe that you have hit your hand. This is a bluff move so make sure that the situation is ripe for a bluff as discussed in Chapter 2.

The Check Raise Draw

At first blush, the check raise draw seems to serve no purpose. We've learned before that with drawing hands, you want to try to draw to the best hand without spending a lot of money. Just calling a bet seems like the more prudent thing to do. Well, let's take a look at how this move can play out.

The Gutshot Straight

You may have seen players on television with various talismans or other fancy card protectors that they place over their card when playing a hand. Those aren't just for show. It's up to each individual player to protect his cards. By using a card protector, you can safeguard against the dealer inadvertently taking your cards or another player errantly tossing his cards on top of yours, which would render your hand dead.

You are in the big blind with Ah4h. A tight aggressive player open raises under the gun and everyone folds to you. You know this player will only raise from early position with a premium hand such as A-K or a big pocket pair. The flop comes 10h6h2d. You have the nut flush draw but are likely behind in the hand.

If you bet, your opponent may put you on the typical big blind move of trying to bet a low flop, and he may raise you. You decide to check and your opponent indeed makes a bet. If you now call, your opponent may suspect you are on a flush draw. If you miss the flush on the turn, he is likely to make a big bet to keep you from drawing to the flush.

However, if you check raise the flop, your opponent is likely to believe you have a homemade hand and are holding cards such as J-10. In that event, your opponent may fold and you've won the hand. Or he may call with a hand like A-K if he believes either an Ace or King will give him a winning hand.

Let's assume he does have A-K. The turn brings the Kh, giving him top pair with top kicker but also making your nut flush. Now, when you bet out, your opponent is likely to raise in the belief that he has the best hand. You can start to see the potential of the check raise draw. The check raise draw gives you the chance to win the pot without drawing to your hand. If you do get called, all is not lost. The nature of your hand is well hidden and you can win a big pot if you make your flush.

Hold 'em

Here's a little tip to help you mix up your play. Before you sit down to the table, pick a time that will occur once an hour for you to play whatever hand you are dealt with strength. If you select "a quarter after," when that hand is dealt after the clock strikes 15 minutes past the hour, play it like you have pocket Aces no matter what cards you receive or what position you are in.

Representing Strength

There are two situations in Hold 'em where bluffs can be routinely successful. All you need is guts and some knowledge about your opponents. Your cards and position are irrelevant. The only thing that matters is the board.

Players are most fearful of seeing an Ace or a flush draw on the flop if it doesn't help them. That's because these hands will frequently help their opponents.

Think about it. Whenever an Ace appears on board, your first thought is that someone just made top pair. Well, that's what your opponents are thinking, too. An Ace is a believable holding for anyone in any position. Raise from early position, it's likely you have A-K. Limp from middle position, you could have A-10. Call a bet from late position, you could have A-3 suited.

When an Ace appears on the flop and your opponent cannot beat a pair of Aces, you stand an excellent chance of winning the pot with a bet or raise because it is very believable that you would have an Ace.

Flushes also scare players because again, it's a believable holding. You could raise with A-K suited from early position, limp with 8-7 suited from middle position, and call with J-10 suited from late position. If two hearts come on the flop, call a bet like you're on a draw. When that third heart hits on the turn, you are in prime position to steal the pot.

These bluffs won't work every time but here are a few tips to maximize your profits:

- Make strong bets or raises but don't risk too much.
- If you get called or raised in your bluff attempt, it's probably best to give up on the hand.
- Never show your cards if you are not called. Since your opponents won't suspect you're bluffing, these moves can be used with a high level of frequency, especially against weak competition.

Sink or Swim

The river is where fortunes are won or lost. A hard-fought hand played to the end with one final round of fighting before the showdown.

Playing the river can be one of the most trying and perplexing moves of poker. Everyone remaining will have a big stake in the pot and the will to fight for it. With all of the cards on the table, the hands are what they are and there will be no more improvement.

Yet this critical point is often where many players throw in the towel. They give up when they miss their draws. They check after leading the betting. They overbet into a hand that just hit a flush. There are many nuances to river play, but we'll try to shed some light on these subtleties with a couple of illustrations.

Fold 'em

In most card rooms, anyone at the table has the right to see the cards of any player at the table who stays in a hand until the river—even if that player loses and intends to muck his cards. Common etiquette, however, is to not ask. What goes around, comes around, so if you ask, expect others to ask to see your cards.

Calling with a Monster

There's a raise and call in front of you and you call in late position with pocket 9s. The flop comes Q-J-10 and you're ready to throw in the towel to any bet. With two other players in the pot, there is an excellent chance someone has a higher pair than yours and possibly even a made straight. To your surprise, the two players in front of you check. This raises your suspicion as you are sure someone must be slow playing a big hand. So you check.

The turn is a 9, giving you a set but also making a straight for anyone holding a K. There's a bet and a call in front of you and you decide to call to see if you make a full house and win a huge pot. The river is another Q. You've made a full house comprised of 999QQ. There's a bet and a call in front of you and just as you reach for your chips dreaming of the big pot you're going to scoop, reality sets in. You replay the hand in your mind and realize that there's a fairly good chance you are beat.

Every hand tells a story, and this one is no different. While one of your opponents may have been slow playing A-K, what does the other one have? The possibilities include K-Q, Q-Q, Q-J, J-J, and 10-10, all of which make bigger full houses than the one you have. There's too much money in the pot not to call, but there is no need to raise. The risk is too great that you will face a big re-raise.

Avoiding Disaster

Let's look at a hand where you open raise from early position with AdKh. You get a call from a player in late position. The flop comes Kd9d2c. With top pair, top kicker, you bet out and your opponent calls. The turn is the 6h. Again, you bet and your opponent calls. You believe your opponent has a hand like K-Q or two diamonds. The river is the 8d, which will make your opponent's flush if he has two diamonds.

What's your move on the river? If your opponent does have the flush, you don't want to bet too much into it. Conversely, if you check, you leave the door wide open for your opponent to bet even if he doesn't have the flush. A small value bet is probably your best option here. You have the Ace of diamonds so you know your opponent cannot have the nut flush. The small value bet may mislead your opponent into thinking you made the better flush and keep him from raising with his flush. In addition, if he does have a hand you beat like K-Q, he is likely to call the smaller bet.

You want to bet a small enough amount that your opponent will still call with a hand that you can beat. If you bet too much, you will only get called or raised by a better hand. Yet, you want the bet big enough so your opponent will be careful about raising with anything other than a high flush. If you do get raised, you can fold your hand with confidence knowing you have been beat. If you had just checked, it would be a lot more difficult to know if you are beat if your opponent bet out since he could be betting either because he has a good hand or in an attempt to steal since you showed weakness.

The Gutshot Straight

Always keep in mind that you are playing poker, not solitaire. Look at the subjective value of your hand, not the objective value. How much your hand is worth can only be measured against the potential strength of your opponents. The action you should take (i.e, whether to check, bet, raise, or fold) depends as much on your opponent's cards as it does yours.

Poker Is Fluid

Poker is an extremely situational game which depends a great deal on your opponents and their style of play. Your opponents will not remain constant. Players will come and go from the table and your opponents will often switch gears throughout their play.

Never sit down to the table with a predetermined idea of how you are going to play. Remain flexible and adjust to what is going on around you. Take the time to reflect on the play of your opponent as well as yourself. If you can master both, victory will be yours.

The Least You Need to Know

- Aces and flushes on the board represent prime bluffing situations.
- Don't get lazy on the river; give a lot of consideration to it, and how much you should bet.
- When playing poker, keep an open mind and be on the lookout for opportunities to exploit.

Glossary

Please note that not all of these terms are used in this book. However, these are all terms that you are likely to hear tossed around at the poker table, so they are included here for your reference.

ace rag In Hold 'em, to have an ace and a card below a 10. Also referred to as Ax.

all-in To place all of one's chips in the pot. To go "all-in" is to bet your entire stack.

ante A set amount of chips that each player (including the blinds) must place in the pot before a hand is dealt. In no-limit Hold 'em tournaments, antes typically are not required until the later rounds.

bad beat Having a strong hand beaten by an opponent who was a big underdog but makes a lucky draw. This is especially true when your opponent is playing poorly and should not have been in the pot in the first place.

best of it Having the best chance of winning the hand at that particular time.

bet, betting To be the first to place chips in the pot on any given round.

big blind Typically that position which is two spots to the left of the button. The big blind must lead the first round of betting with a forced full bet.

big stack Having more chips than the great majority of players at your table.

blank A card that does not help any player.

blind A forced bet that one or two players are force to make to start the first round of betting. The blinds will be the first to act in each subsequent round of betting and, thus, to be in the blind is to be in the unfavorable position. The blinds rotate around the table with each deal and are always to the left of the button.

blinded out To lose your chip stack as a result of posting the mandatory blinds and antes.

bluff A bet or raise made to force your opponent to fold when you sense he is vulnerable even though he may have a better hand.

board The five community cards placed in the center of the table.

button A round disc that rotates around the table with each new deal. The player on the button acts last during each round of betting and, thus, to be on the button is to be in the most favorable position.

buy information   Calling a bet when you are pretty sure you do not have the best hand but you want to find out what cards your opponent was playing.

call   To place in the pot an amount of chips equal to an opponent's bet or raise.

caller   A player who makes a call.

calling station   A weak player who will call just about any bet but will rarely initiate a bet or raise. This type of player is extremely hard to bluff.

chase   To stay in a hand with hopes of outdrawing an opponent with a superior hand.

check   To pass when it is your turn to bet.

check raise   To check and then raise after your opponent bets.

chip   A round token used to represent varying denominations of money.

come over the top   To raise or re-raise with a huge bet.

community cards   The five cards comprising the board which are dealt face up in the center of the table and are shared by all of the players.

covered   This means you have more chips than someone else does.

cutoff   That position which is one to the right of the button and acts right before the button.

draw out   To improve your hand so that it beats a previously superior hand.

drawing dead   Holding a hand that cannot possibly win due to the fact that no matter what card comes up, your opponent will still hold a superior hand.

drawing hand   A hand that has potential but needs help to improve to a winning hand.

early position   Any position in which you will act before most of the other players in a round of betting. In a 10-handed game, the first five positions to the left of the button will be considered early positions.

favorite   A hand that has the best chance of winning at any point in time before all of the cards are dealt.

fifth street   The fifth and final community card in Hold 'em. Also called the river.

flop   The first three community cards, which are all dealt at the same time.

flush   Five cards of the same suit.

fold   To drop out of a hand rather than call a bet or raise.

fourth street   The fourth community card in Hold 'em. Also called the turn.

free card   A card that a player gets to see without having to pay for it. When no one bets on a particular round of playing, the next card is considered a free card.

full house   Three cards of one rank and two of another such as KdKsKc3s3d.

gut shot   An inside straight draw.

heads-up   To play against a single opponent.

hole cards   These are the two unique cards face down that each player is dealt at the beginning.

in the money   In tournament play, only the top finishers will receive prize money. A player who advances to receive prize money is said to have finished in the money.

inside straight draw   A straight which can be completed only by a card of one rank. For example, 3-4-5-7 can only be completed with a 6.

kicker   A side card that is not part of any made hand but can be the deciding factor in determining a winning hand. For example, if you have A-K and your opponent has A-Q, you win on a final board of A-J-8-4-4.

late position   Any position in which you will act after most of the other players in a round of betting. In a 10-handed game, the button and the two positions to the right of the button will be considered late positions.

laydown   To fold your hand in the face of a bet.

levels   Predetermined intervals of play whereby the blinds (and antes, if applicable) will be set for a period of time. The blinds will increase with each level.

limp in To call a bet rather than raise prior to the flop.

loose A player who is playing more hands than he should.

middle pair To pair the second highest card on board.

middle position A position in a round of betting somewhere in the middle. In a 10-handed game, the fourth and fifth position to the right of the button are considered middle positions.

muck To discard a hand without revealing it.

multi-way hand or pot A hand or pot with three or more players.

nut flush The best possible flush hand. For example, if you hold Ad2d and the flop is Jd7d3d, you have the nut flush.

nut flush draw A hand that can improve to the nut flush.

nuts The best possible hand at that point in time.

offsuit Two or more cards of different suits. If you are dealt Jd and 10s, your hand is considered "Jack-Ten offsuit."

on the bubble In tournament play, when players are only a few eliminations away from being in the money. If a player is eliminated in 28th place when 27 places were paid, that player is said to have been eliminated on the bubble.

on tilt To be playing poorly due to a lack of control of your own play.

open-ended straight draw Four cards to a straight, which can be completed by cards of two different ranks. For example, 7-8-9-10 is an open-ended straight draw in that either a Jack or 6 will complete the straight.

outs When you do not have the best hand but there are still more cards to come, those cards that will make your hand a winning hand are called your "outs."

over card(s) To have a card(s) that is higher than any card on the board. If you have KsJd and the flop is Qh4c7s, then you have one over card.

pair Two cards of the same rank, such as 6c, 6h.

pot The collective amount of all chips bet at any point in time.

pot odds The ratio of the amount of chips in the pot to the size of the bet you must call.

put someone on a hand To determine to the best of your ability the hand your opponent is most likely to possess.

rainbow Two to four cards of different suits. If the flop comes 3-6-J rainbow, then there are no two cards of any one suit. For example, 3h6dJs.

raise To bet an additional amount after an opponent makes a bet.

raiser   A player who makes a raise.

rebuy   A rebuy tournament allows a player to rebuy chips for a predetermined amount of time and typically only if the player has less than the original buy-in amount. For example, if a rebuy tournament costs $100 to enter and each player receives 1,000 in chips, players will be allowed to buy an additional 1,000 in chips for another $100 so long as they have less than 1,000 chips at the time of the rebuy. The rebuy option is usually only available for the first three levels of the tournament.

ring game   A single table nontournament game of poker. Also called a side game.

river   The fifth and final community card in Hold 'em.

runner   A card that helps or completes your hand when you need help and that comes on the turn and/or river. For example, you are holding Jh10h and the flop is JsAh2d. Your opponent is holding AdJc. Since no one card will help you, you need two runners in order to win. If the turn is 4h and the river is 9h, you will have hit two runners and made a flush to win the hand.

semi-bluff   To bet with the intention of inducing an opponent with a superior hand to fold, but if he does not, you have a reasonable chance to improve your hand to the best hand.

set   In Hold 'em, three of a kind when you have a pocket pair and the board contains a card of the same rank.

short stacked Playing with a stack of chips that is much smaller than the average chip stack of the other players.

showdown The turning over of all remaining players' cards after the last round of betting is concluded.

side game A single table nontournament game of poker. Also called a ring game.

slow play To not bet or raise with a strong hand in order to trap your opponent and, ultimately, win more chips in the hand.

small blind The small blind position is typically one spot to the left of the button; must post a forced half bet before the cards are dealt.

steal To make a big bet or raise that induces your opponent(s) to fold when you may not have the best hand.

straight Five cards of mixed suits in sequence. For example, AhKdQsJh10c.

suck out To draw a card that improves a hand into a winning one when it had been a big underdog. For example, say you hold 5d6d on a board of 4c7c8h10h and your opponent has KcQc. The river brings the 2c allowing your opponent to make a flush and beat your made straight. Your opponent is said to have sucked out.

suited Two or more cards of the same suit. For example, KdQd.

tell A nuance or mannerism a player may display that gives away his hand.

tight Playing very conservatively or only playing strong hands.

trips Having three cards of the same rank made by using one card from your hand and two cards from the board.

turn The fourth card on the board which is dealt as soon as the betting round following the flop concludes.

under the gun The first player to act on the first round of betting in Hold 'em. Since the blinds have forced bets, the player to the immediate left of the big blind is "under the gun."

underdog A hand that is not the favorite to win.

worst of it Being an underdog to your opponent(s) at that point in time.

Appendix B

Texas Hold 'em Chart of Outs

If you're going to play Texas Hold 'em, you will need to know the odds of making a hand for both you and your opponents. While you don't need to memorize this chart, you should study it until you have a basic feel for the odds shown.

Here is an example: suppose you hold 10h9h and the flop comes Ah5d2h. You are fairly certain that your opponent has an Ace. You are confident, however, that you will win if you can make your flush. What are the odds of making the flush? There are nine other hearts that will make your hand. (Note that there are 13 hearts and you have 2 of them, and 2 more of them showed up on the flop.)

Looking at the chart, we see that you have a 35 percent chance of making your hand if you see it all the way to the river. Expressed in terms of odds, you are a 1.9 to 1 underdog to win. Now, suppose that the turn brings the 8c. You still have those same nine outs. However, with only one card to come, we can see that your chances of winning have decreased dramatically. You now have a 19.6 percent chance of winning and the odds are 4.1 to 1 against you.

Number of outs that will make the hand	After Flop (Two cards to come)		After Turn (One card to come)	
	Percentage chance of making hand	Expressed in Odds (X to 1 against)	Percentage chance of making hand	Expressed in Odds (X to 1 against)
1	4.3	22.4	2.2	44.5
2	8.4	10.9	4.3	22.3
3	12.5	7	6.5	14.4
4	16.5	5.1	8.7	10.5
5	20.3	3.9	10.9	8.2
6	24.1	3.1	13	6.7
7	27.8	2.6	15.2	5.6
8	31.5	2.2	17.4	4.7
9	35	1.9	19.6	4.1
10	38.4	1.6	21.7	3.6
11	41.7	1.4	24	3.2
12	45	1.2	26.1	2.8
13	48.1	1.1	28.3	2.5
14	51.2	0.95	30.4	2.3
15	54.1	0.85	32.6	2.1
16	57	0.75	34.3	1.9
17	59.8	0.67	37	1.7
18	62.4	0.6	39.1	1.6
19	65	0.54	41.3	1.4
20	67.5	0.48	43.5	1.3

Appendix C

Additional Resources

Now you know some fairly solid fundamental play that should get you on a winning path. However, poker is a game of never-ending learning. As you continue to play, I would highly recommend that you supplement your learning curve by reading as many books as possible and taking advantage of some unique online resources. To help you choose from the numerous resources available, here are some recommendations.

Recommended Books

Lessinger, Matt. *The Book of Bluffs*. New York: Warner Books, 2005.

The most detailed book on bluffing available. Matt Lessinger does an excellent job of explaining how there is a science to what is widely viewed as an art form. Filled with excellent samples and analysis, the reader will learn proper bluffing techniques and when to implement them.

Caro, Mike. *Caro's Book of Poker Tells*. New York: Cardoza Publishing, 2003.

The ability to read your opponents will go a long way in helping you decide if and when to bluff and when and how much to bet or raise. Caro's book remains the best on the subject.

Bloch, Andy, and Bobbi Dempsey. *The Pocket Idiot's Guide to Poker Tells*. Indianapolis: Alpha, 2006.

Here's an alternative to Caro's book that gives you thorough information in an easy and entertaining style. Check out this book to get a leg up on the competition.

Sklansky, David. *The Theory of Poker*. Henderson, Nevada: Two Plus Two Publishing, 1994.

This revolutionary book is a treasure trove of valuable information relevant to all of poker. As the title suggests, this book really digs into the purpose of poker and will help you make correct decisions no matter what your game of choice.

Apostolico, David. *Tournament Poker and the Art of War*. Lyle Stuart, 2005.

Okay, so I am biased. Most books teach players the fundamentals and how to play by the book. Once you have that knowledge, you need something more to take your game to the next level. This book applies the principles of Sun Tzu's classic to teach players how to develop the proper mindset to evaluate situations and advance far in tournaments.

Brunson, Doyle. *Super System 2*. New York: Cardoza Publishing, 2005.

Doyle's chapter on no-limit Texas Hold 'em remains the Bible on the subject. His style won't fit everyone, but an understanding of power poker is a must if you want to know proper betting and bluffing techniques.

Esfandiari, Antonio. *WPT: In the Money*. New York: Collins, 2006.

World Poker Tour and World Series of Poker Champion Antonio Esfandiari shares all of his secrets to winning Texas Hold 'em cash games. A great book from a top player that is sure to improve your game.

Online Resources

The last few years have seen a proliferation of websites dedicated to all things poker. Do a Google search to find one you like. Personally, I look for sites that have a broad readership and an active forum for advanced discussion.

I would highly recommend two sites:

- **www.wptfan.com** The (Unofficial) World Poker Tour Fan Site has an open posting policy. While you are likely to come across a number of different topics, there are always some interesting threads discussing specific poker play situations. This site has some very knowledgeable readers who are not afraid to state their opinion.

- **www.twoplustwo.com** This site is run by the people at Two Plus Two Publishing, who put out some of the best poker books on the market. Their website has specific forums for a broad range of poker issues. There are a couple of forums dedicated just to poker strategy, and there is always an active and lively discussion. Post a question and you are sure to get a number of responses.

Of course, as with anything online, be prepared for honest and sometimes harsh advice. Poker players are not afraid to tell it like it is. Of course, you have to be discriminating and weed out the bad from the good.

Poker Sites

Whether you decide to play poker online or for money (I can't advise you either way), there are a few sites that I believe stand out above the others.

- **www.PokerStars.net**   One of the largest and most established, PokerStars offers a full suite of poker games for players of every level.

- **www.PartyPoker.net**   Much like PokerStars in the number of players it attracts and the games offered.

- **www.FullTiltPoker.net**   Not as big as the others, but a well-run site that offers a lot of different games as well as free advice from some of the top players in the world who regularly play there.

Index